transplanted

A MEMOIR

birgit lennertz sarrimanolis

transplanted

birgit lennertz sarrimanolis

Cirque Press
Copyright © 2022 Birgit Lennertz Sarrimanolis

All rights reserved. No part of this publication may be reproduced, distributed or transmitted in any form or by any means, including photocopying, recording, or other electronic or mechanical methods, without the prior written permission of the publisher, except in the case of brief quotations embodied in critical reviews and certain other noncommercial uses permitted by copyright law.

Published by Cirque Press

Sandra Kleven — Michael Burwell
3157 Bettles Bay Loop
Anchorage, AK 99515

Print ISBN: 979-8-89298-976-3

cirquejournal@gmail.com
www.cirquejournal.com

Author photo by Kelly Atlee
Book Design by Emily Tallman, Poetica

To Sarah, for gifting me the rest of my life

AUTHOR'S NOTE

The events described in this book are true. I wrote this book by relying on many personal journals I kept in the years I lived in Alaska. The places in this book exist. For the chronology of events and accuracy of descriptive details, I compared notes with persons that appear in the book. I changed the names and identifying characteristics of most characters in the book. Some names are not fictitious, when their owners graciously granted me permission to include them in the story. For the medical story, I utilized my own medical chart records, researched medical articles and interviewed physicians and nurses. Based on these, I have written the most accurate rendition of the story. While no parts of the story have been fabricated, they have been reconstructed from memory, a tool sometimes imperfect but always true to itself.

CONTENTS

Part One – Taiga and Tundra

1. Autumn Equinox   3
2. Latitude 65   11
3. 7th Floor Northeast   17
4. Birch Hill   23
5. Max   29
6. "Midnight Sun"   33
7. Alaskan Family   37
8. Induction   41
9. Watershed   45
10. Dwindling Counts   49
11. Prisoner of Darkness   53
12. Homestead   57
13. The Factory   63
14. Bad Hair Day   71

Part Two – Permafrost

15. Raven   79
16. Fairbanks at 40° Below   83
17. Aurora Borealis   87
18. 7 plus 3   91
19. Denali Fault Earthquake   95
20. Moon Face   99
21. Thanksgiving Ice Storm   105
22. Remission   109
23. Winter Solstice Fire   111

24. Corridor Walk   *115*
25. Sundogs and Diamond Dust   *121*
26. The Cowbell   *125*
27. Yukon Quest   *129*
28. Neutropenic Fever   *133*
29. The Choice   *139*

Part Three – Arctic Breakup

30. Arctic Breakup   *145*
31. Fifty/Fifty   *151*
32. Chena Ridge Trails   *155*
33. German Women   *159*
34. Seattle Outings   *165*
35. Anniversary Chemo   *171*
36. The Bone Cave   *175*
37. The Parenthesis   *179*
38. Cancer Quilts   *181*
39. The Guardian Tree   *185*
40. Bedtime Story   *187*
41. Letter from My Donor   *191*
42. Seattle Sunshine   *195*
43. Chimera   *203*

Epilogue – Beyond Boreas   *207*

PART ONE

Taiga and Tundra

"Taiga," Alaska's boreal forest, is comprised of spruce, birch and aspen. A landscape of mountains, meadows, marshes, lakes and rivers covers the Far North.

Hindered by winters that are long and cold, a treeless "tundra" blankets the mountains and valleys further north, where only low shrubs, mosses and lichens grow.

CHAPTER ONE
Autumn Equinox

I wrapped myself fiercely in my blanket and looked stonily at Andrew, my oncologist, then at Nick, my husband, also a doctor. Both wore vexed faces. And green scrubs. Andrew pulled up a chair to sit down close to the bed. He leaned forward, dead earnest, and I knew then that Nick had asked him to return to the house with him to deliver the news and to outline my black prognosis. I felt Andrew's warm hand covering my icy one. Nick, standing next to him, was eerily composed. His face was bone white. I sensed he was exercising his utmost restraint to not break down in front of me. This time, their patient was a friend, a wife.

I thought it unusual to hear tires crunching down the snowy driveway in the middle of the day on a Tuesday. I had been resting beneath the slanting eaves of our bedroom. The light was already fading mid-afternoon, a darkness that quickly cloaked the outlines of spruces and the stark branches of the birches on the hill. The children were at school and Nick was in town working in his practice. The house was still, not soothingly, but more in a silence that was empty of everything. The sound of shutting car doors and the churning mechanism of the garage door came abruptly, amplified and echoing through the house. I recognized my husband's muffled voice downstairs, then Andrew's. One day we would invite our guests into the house through the front door rather than through the garage, where they wouldn't stumble over our winter boots untidily strewn near the door.

Why were they both here? Did doctors still make house calls? I was immediately uneasy. When they shuffled into my bedroom, their expressions told the story long before their words did. My palms had already gone sweaty.

"We got the bone marrow biopsy results," Andrew said, head lowered as he leaned in, voice low. "There are still eighty percent of leukemic cells present in your body."

I sat, petrified. *Eighty percent!* The chemotherapy round I endured had done little to improve my condition. The medicines had exerted no impact on the disease's hostility, no counterblow. My breath stalled. Propped up against the pillows on the bed, I focused on the two doctors by my side, trying to grasp the meaning of his words. Through the rush of blood in my ears, I thought I dimly heard Andrew again.

"We can start comfort measures. You don't need to experience any pain."

I heard the frightened thudding of my own heart. Time passed. I couldn't tell how long Andrew sat by my side. Then Nick's hand grasped mine.

"Things may go south," he whispered, mask gone, features etched with distress.

I stared at him. He was my rootedness. My equilibrium. All of a sudden, my mind spun like a compass without direction, jumpy needle uncontrolled.

"Is there no hope?" I pleaded, my gaze locked and urgent, but something had already crumbled inside me.

My husband's voice was quiet, diminished with futility and grief. "There is always hope."

On the autumn equinox, four weeks earlier, the saturated colors of fall had spread through the Alaskan tundra. The lichen had turned white and the tundra bright orange. The fireweed, already bloomed, was silver among the deep purple of the wild iris. The Tanana River, grey with glacial sediment, wove its way through the broad Tanana Valley. In the far distance, the contours of the snow-capped mountains of the Alaska Range, angular and razor sharp and white, dominated the horizon. It was a colorful tapestry, extravagant in hue, yet short-lived in duration.

For a day, the earth was held in balance between night and day. Equal amounts of daylight and night were poised as the sun crossed the celestial equator, rising precisely in the east, setting perfectly in the west. And then, the constant faltered. The sun continued to descend as night took over. The coming winter beckoned with a time of darkness.

Like most people living in Alaska, I prepared a checklist for the autumn cleanup. Winter comes early, often unexpectedly, to interior Alaska. I sensed the brittleness of the air through my nose and knew it was only a matter of days before snow flurries would fly. The first hard frost stiffened the earth that morning. This year, I vowed, I would be ready for it.

I busied myself with smaller chores: stacking away deck furniture, removing garden hoses, dragging gardening tools – wheelbarrow, trowels, whisky barrel planters – over to the woodshed. Whatever I didn't know what to do with I concealed beneath a large blue tarp. Walking around the house, I eyed the roof for loose shingles, checking the windows for cracks in the casings. In the tool closet, I looked through our emergency kit – duct tape, rope, flashlights, blankets, whistles, food with a longer shelf life, water bottles, a signal mirror—all still intact. In the garage, the cars' summer tires still needed to be changed over to Blizzaks.

For larger endeavors, I sought out Eddie and Rusty. Eddie, the fireman, was busy all summer dousing remnant wildfires that rose sporadically throughout the taiga forests, triggered by lightning or inattentive campers. In the winter, Eddie worked at odd jobs; clearing leaves out of rain gutters and cutting away spindly aspen branches that could fall onto the roof during a winter storm. The whirring and brum, brum, brum of his chainsaw sounded all day, followed by the thump of logs being stacked in the woodshed behind the house. Rusty, who supplemented his income by snowplowing in the winter, came to ask about our plowing needs. We stood near the top of the driveway and looked at the steep slope down towards the house. We mapped how he would plow us out and where to scrape the snow berm to its height as the winter progressed.

"Maybe we won't get quite as much snow as last winter," Rusty joked, his complexion ruddy and red. I grinned back. Snowfall in Fairbanks was always guaranteed. He hauled a generator into the garage, explaining the hook-up maneuvers to me. This way, I would be ready if the power failed in subzero temperatures.

I finished gathering the last of the flowerpots, my meager summer attempt at taming the Alaskan landscape. I threw the withered remains of petunias and dahlias into the encroaching willows behind our house. By the end of August, the seasons were already transitioning. The leaves of the willows and birches had turned ochre and crimson. The tips of the feathery fireweed nodded in the breeze, ready to be carried away. Wild rosehips shriveled in the crisper air. Not far above me, the remaining leaves of the aspens quavered and twitched in the wind. The wilderness was raw. There was no quelling or domestication of this landscape. It always had the upper hand.

A sudden, shooting stab of pain in my back made me wince. I sat, abruptly, on a log from the woodpile, inhaling sharply. I could smell the musky scent of the high bush cranberries that grew along the incline of our gravel driveway. At my feet, the fallen birch leaves looked trodden. Straightening slowly, I left the wooden chairs and table which I had been stacking in a heap and went indoors.

"I've strained my back somehow," I told Nick, cringing.

Nick glanced up from the *Annals of Internal Medicine* journal he was absorbed in. He was always reading up on his patients' medical conditions, even after he finished work at his practice. Slanting light fell through the window onto the wooden dining room table. Sheets of paper were spread out, fan like, in front of him. Surfacing, it took him a moment to register my comment.

"Have you tried taking Tylenol? Or doing some stretches?" he mumbled before turning his attention back to his journal article.

I turned from him, placing my hands onto the hollow of my back, rotating my hips one way, then the other, stretching out my crooked posture. Did I twist sharply while stacking the garden furniture? I felt no quick jerk in movement, no awkward strain, just the sudden pain. I rummaged in the kitchen cabinet for Acetaminophen and tried to shrug off my discomfort.

The pain remained and grew steadily as the weekend drew to a close. By Sunday evening I could not contain it any longer.

"It's getting worse!" I said to Nick, walking about the house as though I was bridging labor pains. This time, Nick watched me critically.

Darkness descended early that night. Yanni and Helen, our children, sat with the remainder of their Sunday evening homework at the kitchen counter. Helen was charting everything in our refrigerator and kitchen pantry into a food pyramid for her science assignment. Fruits, vegetables, oils, sweets.

"Is corn a vegetable or a grain, Mom?"

I angled my back into a curve to make the pain subside. My answer came haltingly. Yanni, brow furrowed, was engrossed in his algebra homework: integers and number lines and graphs. He had not even heard us.

The pain in my limbs escalated. It crept from my back to my shoulder blades and around to the front of my chest. I hauled myself up the stairs and went to bed even before the children that evening. All night I thrashed and turned. Perspiration plastered my hair to my forehead. The pain racked my limbs and torso. I woke Nick, who sat up in a start, focusing. He rubbed a hand through his tousled hair and stared at me. Collecting himself, he brought me a washcloth, another Tylenol with a glass of water, some calming words. I drifted off for a while.

Morning dawned numb and grey. Earlier, I heard Nick and the children downstairs, as he prepared their breakfast while I tried to gather the energy to get out of bed. He drove them to school and returned before I had even heaved myself into the bathroom. Exhausted, I sat on the edge of the bathtub to brush my teeth.

When I changed out of my pajamas, I saw great splotches, mauve and brown bruises, had developed on my body overnight. It looked as though I had been beaten in a bar brawl. I stared at the patterns on my legs, prodding them with my finger. There was no sensation, no feeling at all. I cried out to Nick, horrified.

I was still wearing my pajamas when Nick rushed me into the car.

"Don't bother changing clothes," he insisted. "We have to go now!"

He drove down the Chena Ridge Road at breakneck speed, glancing at me from time to time. The birch trees along the road were ravished in yellow and auburn. I tried counting empty spaces between them.

In the emergency room of Fairbanks Memorial Hospital, a nurse drew blood. Sounds came from beyond the curtained partitions: the shuffle in and out of patients' cubicles, groans, muted voices, the pump of a blood pressure cuff. My nerves were strung tight. I waited for the next thing to happen, another bit of information, an explanation. I sensed that it would not bring relief. When I saw Andrew approaching me, my heart froze. His presence as an oncologist could mean only one thing. I knew my diagnosis of cancer before he had even uttered the words "acute myeloid leukemia."

After the initial whirling in my head subsided a little, fuzziness took its place. I grappled with the enormity of the situation. An immense numbness overtook me then, perhaps due to the Oxycodone the nurse had given me earlier to alleviate the shooting stabs in my back. The room around me looked frayed.

"Are we absolutely sure of the diagnosis?" Nick, his face ashen, spoke urgently to Andrew. His voice was strained in desperation, an octave higher than usual, in his last effort to change the roll of the dice.

Andrew's face reddened, not because he was insulted, but because he must have felt his friend's agony. They had worked together for many years, referring patients to each other, consulting on maladies, discussing lab results. Neither had ever encountered the position he found himself in this morning.

"The pathologist is concerned as well," Andrew said quietly.

He turned to me. "Do you understand what I am saying?"

Oddly enough, I had no tears, no exclamation of disbelief, no frantic denial. I simply looked at him, stunned.

A single, simple blood test made the world careen and go shapeless. My white blood cells, which fight infections, were above the normal range. My platelets, which help clot blood, were well below. They should have been in a normal range above 150,000 per microliter of blood, I heard him say. Mine hovered at a mere 6,000. The test had detected blasts, immature white blood cells, in my bloodstream. All confirmed acute leukemia.

Time collapsed. Different people materialized at different moments. I could not tell whether minutes or hours had passed. Suddenly, Yanni and Helen stood next to my bed in the emergency room cubicle, their large eyes dark and lustrous with frightened tears.

"The news is not good this morning," I told them with a watery smile, mustering an ounce of bravery. "I need to stay in the hospital so the pain in my back will get better."

I could not bring myself to say the words "cancer" or "leukemia" to them. I could not even accept the words myself. I shook my head in disbelief. The disease had been ruthless and quick in its descent upon our lives.

Then, the children were gone and my friends, Rebecca and Tara, hovered by my bed, blinking. Their talking was braided, their words bumping into each other.

"I must say you have put just the tiniest wrinkle into my Monday morning," Rebecca tried to feebly joke. More earnestly, she said "I came straight from work when I heard."

"I found you on my own," Tara said. "I didn't even wait for the nurse to show me in." Her face was blotched, a trace of earlier tears.

Their efforts were directed at making conversation at a time when talking was impossible.

"The Medical Center in Seattle specializes in leukemias of all sorts," Andrew was explaining to Nick, standing near the door behind my friends. "I will make preparations for the transport tomorrow morning."

I looked at him, bewildered. I hadn't even known there were different types of leukemia. All I knew about leukemia was that it affected blood cells and that its outcome was almost always calamitous. Leukemia afflicted others, not me. I was healthy. I cross-country skied in the winter months along trails that wound through the woods, across frozen Smith Lake. I could swim for a mile and a half in an hour. I was able to run distances. I started the running season early, when snow patches still dotted the hills and I sloshed my running shoes through the puddles. I was well conditioned physically, robust and strong. Leukemia came to fictitious people in movies: "Dying Young" and "Love Story" and "My Sister's Keeper." Or to people for whom donations were gathered in collection jars at gas stations or whose faces peered from pamphlets pinned to bulletin boards, invitations to a fund-raising spaghetti feed. All this was always at a comfortable distance from myself. How could leukemia have possibly found its way to me?

I couldn't grasp the situation, although its urgency was clear, that much I gathered from Andrew, Nick, the nurses, my friends. My condition was critical. It was not uncommon for Alaskan patients to seek medical attention in Anchorage or Seattle or even farther away. But a Medevac flight to Seattle? The very next day?

I was transported to Seattle in a small ambulance aircraft. Two young, muscular men that looked more like ice hockey players than paramedics lifted the gurney into the airplane's interior. The space was confined, crammed with CPR equipment, ventilators, monitoring units. I was cognizant of Nick's presence behind me in the narrow airplane interior, but I couldn't see him because of the restricting gurney straps. I vaguely wondered who was taking care of Yanni and Helen. I had always been a nervous flyer, gathering my inner strength to step over the threshold between terminal walkway and open airplane door. Countless times in the past, when it came time to board an aircraft, I pulled Nick aside the night before our flight.

"We'll be alright, don't you think?" I asked him softly, so the children would not hear.

"The chances of the airplane going down is one in a million," he jested, his eyes twinkling.

Weren't those same statistics true of developing leukemia?

I listened to the paramedics talk to the pilot through the narcotic fog developing around me. I couldn't swallow beyond the dryness in my throat. It was, indeed, possible to be struck with the unlikely, the unimaginable. As the airplane took off, I could see the sprawling tundra and taiga forests of the Tanana Valley through the small oval window. The Alaskan landscape tilted before the earth fell away beneath me.

CHAPTER 2
Latitude 65

Ten years before, my very first glimpse of Alaska had also been from above. It was winter, January of 2001. Our Alaska Airlines flight from Seattle to Anchorage hurtled north. The thrill of seeing this unknown land firmly suppressed my fear of flying. Instead of tingling nervousness, I felt a whoosh of blood in my ears. We were really going, in the dead of winter, to Fairbanks in Alaska's forbidding interior.

We flew north for hours, over snow-capped mountains that stretched endlessly in all directions. Peering down, I saw no towns, roads or signs of habitation. Only the jaggedness of mountain peaks and striated, purple glaciers curving along valleys, inching their way forward under the pressure of their own weight. It was an immeasurable space, a vastness without edges.

We spoke, some weeks earlier, about a change.

"Have you ever thought about living elsewhere?" In recollection, I wasn't sure whether it was Nick or I that asked the question.

We lived in Ohio for a decade, a life that had become complacent and anticipated. We acclimated to the town, the neighborhood, the gentle swell of country roads through wavering, golden cornfields. We worked as young professionals paving our careers. Nick was a resident doctor. I worked in the education department of an art center. Nick sat in examining rooms with patients, listening to their complaints, evaluating their health. I organized teacher workshops and trained tour guides and developed interpretive gallery sessions for school children. When Nick joined a medical practice in bucolic Bellefontaine, an hour's drive from Columbus, we bought a house with a wraparound porch, a copse of trees in the back garden and a view down the incline of Reservoir Road. Walking hand in hand along the quiet streets in the evenings, we listened to the pines that whispered and swayed, the trees after which the neighborhood was named. Afterwards, sitting on our porch swing, we watched the evening light slowly surrender. We saw our lives unfold in our minds. It was comfortable and graspable. Content, we never questioned leaving.

Until, one day, for no reason better than the next, an itch burrowed itself. We wanted to look beyond the customary, to follow an urge to try something wilder, something unbridled and new.

Nick's voice sounded muffled through the closed bathroom door. He was reading the latest *New England Journal of Medicine*.

"There is an ad here for the Tanana Valley Clinic. In Fairbanks, Alaska. They are looking for an internist."

I stared at him when he came out of the bathroom. What did we know about Alaska? A Last Frontier, an enormous, mostly unpopulated land one-fifth the size of America. Living conditions were inhospitable. Darkness prevailed. Temperatures reached 70° below zero in the winter. Eskimos lived in igloos. Huskies were harnessed to sleds. Moose and bears roamed freely. It was a land of extremes: in temperature, in mountain peaks, in survival means, in size. Nick and I looked at each other. We knew our facts were flawed and our perspective stereotyped. Our enthusiasm, however, was immediately and firmly cemented. With a shiver of excitement, I grasped Nick's hand. We could shape our future. We were in control of our lives. At the time, we both believed this.

An intercom announcement alerted us to the fact that the airplane was slowly descending. I caught sight of Alaska. I tugged on Nick's sleeve and drew in my breath. Anchorage lay below, at the far end of Cook Inlet. The sharp, snow-covered peaks of the Chugach Mountains rose into low, dark clouds. The light, at midday, was metallic. Great floes of ice lay on the water. Alaska. I read the name stemmed from the Aleut word *alaxsxaq*. A great land. One that the sea breaks against.

"We will be parking the aircraft a short distance from the terminal." I glanced up at the nasal voice of the flight attendant over the intercom. "All passengers are requested to walk across the tarmac to the airport building,"

I collected my bag from the overhead bin and pulled my coat closer, equipping myself for a blast of polar air. I waited anxiously for the door to open. When I stepped outside and slowly took in the winter air, it did not penetrate my lungs sharply or send me into coughing fits as I had expected. It felt cold and damp, having been carried in from the sea, but it was not cutting. I was almost disappointed.

Later, sitting at the airport gate awaiting our next flight into the interior, I brightly commented on this to a man sitting nearby. His face was unshaven, his skin wrinkled beneath a baseball cap that advertised a local pipefitters union. I caught a whiff of sour body odor.

"Anchorage is always milder than Fairbanks," he grunted when I told him our destination. "Fairbanks is colder than a ditch digger's toes in the Klondike."

He pulled his cap down over his eyes, dropped his head down to his chest and crossed his arms. Clearly, our conversation was over. I was left pondering about our destination, my heartbeat quickening.

I took in the people around us. In the middle of winter, there were few tourists. Most people wore sensible clothing, adapted to the northern climate: Carhartt pants, fleece, hats, boots. Alaskans were a motley assortment of types, I decided. I could not rely on appearances to figure out anyone's profession or income level. I wondered what had brought them north.

Our flight to Fairbanks was only forty-five minutes. We took our seats in a foreshortened cabin. Half of the cabin's space was partitioned off for cargo. A flight attendant, despite the rush of a brief flight, paused to explain.

"We sometimes transport cargo and provisions even on commercial flights. Alaska is so vast. Supplies need to be delivered to bush communities."

Our airplane, we learned, was flying on to Utqiagvik, the northernmost settlement in Alaska on the Arctic Coast. It was a place so far north that it would not see another sunrise until early spring.

Nick and I drove our rental car tautly down streets that were white and frozen solid beneath a layer of packed snow, following the directions from the parking attendant at the airport.

"It's a straight shot down Airport Way," he told us. "Nothing is far in Fairbanks. Take a left on Noble Street and you'll see the only six-storied structure on that street. That's the clinic."

Darkness had descended even though it was barely four in the afternoon. The temperature dropped noticeably. We peered through the gloom at our surroundings. Fairbanks was a low, sprawling frontier town along the Chena River. It felt like an outpost even though its population ranked it Alaska's second largest city. It stood, on the edge of impinging wilderness, as the last larger municipality before a rough, far-reaching, predominantly uninhabited hinterland.

Downtown Fairbanks was little more than a few office buildings, a couple of hotels, a few eateries, a bank. A bridge crossed the Chena River where I could make out the outlines of a white clapboard church. Souvenir shops, catering to summer tourists, lined the sidewalks. On display in the store front window were ulu knives and stuffed huskies and gold flakes suspended in pendants. The store attendant, sitting behind the counter, looked bored. A handful of pedestrians walked at a brisk pace, hats pulled down, muffled in scarves, dodging into the next office building or business. On Cushman Street, some locals had gathered in a coffee shop, peering out at the cars.

Small houses, some built of log, lined the side roads. They looked like leftovers from the gold prospecting days. Arctic entries, transitional spaces that demarcated a space for shedding outdoor clothing, were crammed with snow shovels, winter boots, and parkas. Windows, small and deeply embedded, withstood extreme temperatures. A heavy snow blanket covered tight gardens.

We located the clinic, a square, unpretentious, grey building on Noble Street where Nick would interview with clinic administrators the following morning. We spent that night at the Fairbanks Princess Hotel near the outskirts of town, on the banks of the frozen Chena River. The hotel receptionist handed us a room key card.

"You better plug in tonight. Otherwise, you might not have much of a start in the morning."

We left our rental car on a parking lot that was lined with outlets. Parked cars drew power through plugged-in extension cords. The cars were equipped with an engine block heater and a battery and oil pan blanket. When activated, these northern adaptations warmed up the engine and kept the motor oil viscous. The temperature would plummet drastically in the night. Without precautions, hydraulics could stall.

My stomach tingled as a pulse of excitement rushed through my body. The night would be so cold that cars would start sluggishly in the morning. In the icebox outside, even spit could turn to ice before it hit the ground, the hotel clerk told us with a grin.

We ate dinner in the loft of the hotel beneath an enormous, antlered moose head. Afterwards, I put on long johns underneath my jeans and my heavy winter coat. I wrapped a scarf around my neck and pulled on mittens. I wanted to go outside. I simply had to feel it for myself.

The night air was piercing. Without the regulating influence of an ocean nearby, the dry cold of interior Alaska was extreme. I quickly realized that my clothing, suitable for winter in Ohio, was no measure for the deep freeze of Fairbanks. The hairs in my nostrils tickled as they froze. Darkness extended around me beneath an inky sky full of twinkling stars. Snow reflected the moonlight brightly, soft and violet, and I had little difficulty seeing. I made my way, boots crunching, down the snow packed lane behind the hotel to the river's edge.

The ice bridge is what the hotel attendant had called it.

"But don't drive over it with a larger vehicle just yet," she warned. "The ice is only eight or nine inches thick."

The ice on the Chena River was dusted with the most recent snowfall. Black spruce grew on the banks of the far side. I stood for some time, inhaling air that smelled of wet spruce. The quiet was enveloping. Suddenly I saw the headlights of a car on the river as it negotiated its way across the ice. My heart hammered. The car, haltingly, maneuvered slowly across the river ice, then bumped its way over the snow berm on the riverbank onto the snowy lane. I let out the breath I was holding. That night, frayed from travel and saturated with first impressions, I slept for hours without moving.

Morning dawned on a cerulean sky. I took in my surroundings, which I had only observed in darkness the day before. The snow, tightly packed, glittered. It was of the purest white I had ever seen. Spruce trees grew in abundance, contrasting with the pristine whiteness. Beyond the river, forested, snow-covered hills rose on the edges of town. The air crackled crisp and dry. Buoyant, I drew in my breath. Alaska brimmed with possibilities.

CHAPTER 3

7th *Floor Northeast*

We did not have the luxury of time. The hurried aircraft transport to Seattle, the waiting ambulance in the hangar with its flashing lights, the paramedics standing by, all were marked by a sense of urgency. The "hockey player" flight paramedic who sat beside me for the duration of the flight, adjusting the nasal oxygen cannula back into my nose whenever I shifted, helped load my stretcher from airplane to ambulance. He paused only for the briefest moment to give my shoulder a gentle squeeze. Then the ambulance doors slammed shut.

I had just arrived in my room on the seventh floor of the University of Washington Medical Center when a medical team – attending physician, resident doctor, and two trailing medical students – filed into my room. They lined up in front of the bulletin board at the end of the bed. Doctors in long white lab coats. Students in shorter ones. All wore grave demeanors.

"We need to discuss the chemo regimen we intend to use," Dr. Eakins, the attending doctor of the team, said without preamble.

He was a small man with round glasses and silvery hair. Had I met him in the hallway, I would never have ascribed to him his senior rank in the hospital. I was referred to him in particular because he was a leading authority on leukemia, part of the renowned Cancer Care Alliance in Seattle. He propped a small laptop onto the tray table next to my bed and logged in. After consulting a table, he turned to Nick and me.

"It is a combination of Clofarabine, Cytarabine and Filgrastim," he told us. "The regimen is called G-CLAC."

Hovering in a haze, I tried to concentrate on his words. He spoke in a foreign language. The narcotic painkillers I had been given had temporarily dulled the pain radiating throughout my body. The side effect was that my thoughts were sluggish, as though they were being dredged from a swamp, mud sucking.

I tried to snap into focus. Dr. Eakins spoke of certain markers that measured the aggressiveness of the leukemia and the likelihood that chemotherapy might even counteract the disease. He proposed a particular combination of medicines that he believed would have an impact on the diseased cells carousing through my veins. Nick asked questions, his features slate gray. Faintly, I heard him ask about the risks and benefits of the trial drugs. They spoke of alternate chemotherapy drugs with names such as Fludarabine and Idarubicin. I heard them mention B cells and T cells. The amount of blast cells in my bloodstream came to 33 percent.

I was unmoored. I did not understand the medical terminology. Drained, I looked out of the window instead. My room overlooked a canal, bordered on the far side by waterfront houses and large, drooping willows. Anchored motorboats bobbed peacefully in the quiet canal. Beyond them the city rose along low hills, veiled in a mist of rain. To the east, a bridge with two towers crossed an expanse of water. The sound of traffic below was muted. I later learned that the air on the entire hospital floor was regulated by HEPA filters. They screened out not only possible contaminants but also the sounds of life outside.

"Your condition is critical," Dr. Eakins did not mince his words. "We need to act immediately." He handed me consent forms to sign. "You'll be enrolled in a clinical trial. Protocol 7144. You are a good candidate for this."

His expression turned stone serious. "It is a trial combination of medicines. There are no guarantees. We will simply have to go through the regimen and see."

I looked to Nick and saw a battle of thoughts race through his mind. He was still, fingers laced, brow knitted. I could tell he was weighing in the pros and cons.

"I think we need to go ahead with it," he told me, quiet but resolute. He took my hand. His presence had always carried weight. I did not have the stamina to reflect or argue. I signed the consent forms without reading them.

A nurse entered the room as the medical team filed out. She wore pink scrubs that offset her dark hair and olive skin. Her large, dark eyes were her best feature.

"My name is Ruth." she smiled broadly. "I'm the head nurse assigned to your care. This is Steven. He is in training on the oncology-hematology floor."

Steven materialized behind her. In contrast to Ruth, he was lanky, red-haired and fair skinned. His smile was a little droopy.

Ruth pulled on a pair of purple latex gloves. She checked the IV line that the paramedics in Fairbanks had inserted into my left hand, securing the needle with bright blue tape. I sensed her proficiency and competence. Ruth spoke as she worked, explaining her actions, for Steven's benefit and for my comfort. There was time for nothing but practicalities.

"Take this," Ruth handed me a pill of Ambien and a water bottle. "It will help you relax."

"I hear you live in Alaska," she continued, conversationally. "What's it like so far north?"

I wished I had the energy to tell her about Alaska. But I felt extinguished.

"Nice," I said, dully.

Ruth smiled at me. "You're scheduled to have a Hickman port placed later today," she said. "Has anyone explained what that is to you?"

I shook my head, alarmed.

"It is a device that is temporarily implanted in your chest," she calmly explained. "It's like an IV that doesn't need to be removed and can stay in your body for several months. That way we don't have to poke you all the time."

Months? I squirmed to prop myself up. I couldn't stay in the hospital for months!

Ruth patted my arm and told me to get some rest. She would return later to check on me. I swallowed the pill and laid back on the pillows. Every muscle in my body bunched. I looked to Nick, who sat in an armchair by the window, waxen faced. He was rubbing a crease from his forehead.

"This is beating me up inside," he told me. "I knew about your anemia from your lab work a year ago, but I didn't follow up on it."

I remained silent.

"I thought it was due to your menstrual cycle," he continued. "Or you not eating meat very often. You were only mildly anemic. I would have never thought it was leukemia."

I was not sure how to respond.

"How is it I pick up on everyone's disease except yours?"

He stood up and walked over to the window, peering blindly at the raindrops trickling down the pane. When he turned, perplexed and tormented, he whispered, "I dropped the ball on my own wife."

I was confounded. My blood cells had started mutating a year ago. Without visible symptoms the disease had infiltrated stealthily over many months. While I carried on—teaching at the university, driving the children to school, preparing dinner in the evenings—an uncontrolled replication of cells was taking place in my bone marrow. Proteins were dividing and propagating. My DNA was changing. Control had gone awry. The only warning sign was a slightly lower red blood cell count on a CBC lab test, easily ascribed to iron deficiency, or a lowered Vitamin B12 level, or mild anemia. Only when the horrifying symptoms of the last weekend emerged did we realize the diagnosis was much more.

I wanted to say something to Nick but couldn't find my voice. It was the most I could do to concentrate on something little, something concrete, to just keep breathing from one moment to the next without disintegrating.

In the dark hours of the early morning, a medical orderly wheeled me through endless hospital corridors. His face, from my vantage point below, looked abbreviated. His nose loomed large. A shock of black hair fell over his forehead. Tiled walls traveled by. The polished floors gleamed under fluorescent lights. The scent of disinfectant hung in the air. The orderly spoke of trivialities. I heard only snippets of the conversation.

"I spent a summer in Alaska once," he told me as we passed through several double doors that he opened automatically by pressing levers on the wall. He had worked at an onshore cannery for a season, processing salmon that traveled up Ketchikan Creek during the spawning season to lay their eggs.

"The hours were long," he described the seasonal work. "But the pay good." He continued talking, not aware that I was tuning out. "I was in charge of barreling and crating the salmon after the fish had gone through the slime line. You wouldn't believe the sheer number of salmon that came through."

Salmon swam against the stream for hundreds of miles from the ocean, up inland rivers, jumping up rocky waterfalls, defying the paws of swiping bears on the banks to end up where they were born. Once there, they spawned for one last time to secure the next generation and then died. An incredibly unquestioned and destined life cycle.

I didn't know which was more surreal: me being wheeled into an operating room in a Seattle hospital or the orderly telling me about his summer job crating fish in Alaska. I had never been to Ketchikan, a small town located on an island in Southeast Alaska in the Tongass National Forest, but I had heard of the picturesque, stilted boardwalks and colorful storefronts at the water's edge. It was a popular destination for cruise ships during the summer months. I read about the totem poles carved by the Tlingits from cedar embodying their ancestry and traditions. I had always longed to see them.

In the operating room the orderly shifted me from the gurney onto a narrow operating bed. I shivered at the sudden change in temperature. Then a surgeon with piercing blue eyes loomed over me. A mask covered the lower half of his face and a green cap was pulled over his hair.

"We need to place a central line that leads to the main vein going into your heart," he explained without introducing himself. "I will make a small incision into your chest and feed the line under the subclavian bone into the superior vena cava. Two small tubes will dangle on the outside of your chest when I am done."

I blinked.

"It's called a Hickman Port. Chemotherapy drugs are toxic. This way, we'll be able to give you medicines and fluids through the port rather than peripheral veins."

I shuddered before drifting off into a dreamless sleep.

I awoke in my hospital room. Nick sat huddled in the armchair. The nightstand clock blinked 4:30 in the morning. Dark circles smudged his eyes. He had not slept in the past three days either.

CHAPTER 4
Birch Hill

In June, the sun in Alaska had no intention of setting. Around midnight it sank closer to the horizon, casting a diffuse light over Fairbanks and the surrounding tundra and taiga forests only to rise again a few hours later, following a shallow arc over the Alaska Range on the horizon. Under the endless hours of daylight, the vegetation exploded into tangles of color. The spruce forests were thick. The meandering rivers looked swollen.

I stood with Yanni, our baby of a year and a half, on my hip. The tarmac was hot with the evening sun. I followed the other passengers across the tarmac into the terminal of the Fairbanks airport. In the baggage claim area, a huge grizzly bear, preserved by taxidermists in a glass case, stood tall in greeting. Tour guides held signs: Princess Tours, Alaska Land and Sea, Chena Hot Springs Resort. Summer tourists who had just disembarked from the airplane from Seattle were hauling luggage from the conveyer belt: backpacks, duffle bags, fishing poles, ice coolers securely fastened with duct tape. I smiled. It was summer in Alaska.

Nick, in khaki shorts and a baseball cap, pushed his way through the crowd. "Finally!" He beamed. He embraced the baby and me at the same time. "We're all here."

After accepting the position offered to him by the Tanana Valley Clinic, Nick gave his partners at the medical practice in Bellefontaine six months' notice. The time was needed to accommodate for his replacement and to prepare ourselves for the Alaskan adventure we were embarking on. In early June we loaded a rented Penske truck, cramming into it our accumulated belongings of a decade's living in Ohio. Bed sheets, cutlery, dinner plates, clothing. The comfortable couch that had survived many evenings of leisure reading and a basement flooding. Stacks of books which we could not bear to part with. Boxes of wine that had reached a perfect age and ruby red color after careful cultivation in Nick's wine cellar. Artifacts from our travels. The Egyptian copper plate, etched with Arabic inscriptions, bought at the Khan-el-Khalili bazaar in Cairo. The Balinese batik, the wax application on the textile still tangible, depicting the ancient mythological story of Gods and demons. The Amish quilt we found in a roadside store in the small town of Charm in Ohio.

With our belongings rattling in the back of the Penske truck and hauling our car behind it on a trailer, Nick drove up the Alcan Highway. For days he traveled through Indiana and Illinois and Iowa, to the Dakotas, on to Montana and up through Canada, finally arriving in Alaska.

Yanni and I gave him a head start of two weeks. I wrapped up the sale of our house in Bellefontaine, selling the last bits of furniture and leftovers that did not fit into the moving truck. They were things we believed we would find little use for in Alaska: patio furniture and umbrella, a kiddie swimming pool, roller blades, high heeled shoes.

Nick's eyes shone after embracing us in the bustle at the airport, brimming with vignettes of what he had encountered along the Alaska Highway. Eager as I was to hear, we had to find time for them later. Yanni, glassy eyed after the long journey, bellowed out a long howl.

We drove through town and followed the Steese Highway north. Willows stood tall, swaying along the roadway. Bluebells, white dwarf dogwood and wild geraniums dotted the meadows near Farmer's Loop Road. On Birch Hill, paper birch and white spruce grew in each other's shadows. We drove down Concord Drive, a winding road that led into the woods. The houses, set back from the road, were scattered apart from each other. In the clearings between them, fireweed grew in spiky, purple clusters, slowly blossoming up their stalks. We bumped along the graveled road for a mile or two before we reached the Dawson's house.

The apartment we had rented occupied the lower level of their home. The rooms were oriented around a central staircase, closed off by a door to the Dawson's living areas above. The inner walls were convexly curved around the stairs, giving a billowing effect. There were two bedrooms; one faced north, the other west. In between were a living area with a fireplace, a dining niche in the kitchen, a bathroom and a storage area. It was sparse yet sufficient.

I thankfully settled Yanni into his crib, which Nick had already assembled, and drew the curtain against the sun still high in the sky. Tiptoeing out, I went to stand by the large living room window that looked out onto the clearing. The lime green of the paper birch trees surrounding the house shimmered in the evening light. Fluid, silvery light had settled in between the branches. I exhaled.

The Dawson family that lived upstairs was friendly and numerous. Tim and Tessa had come to Alaska with the military. After some years he retired, moved off base and found a job at a used car dealership. Together with Tessa, he built the house in the woods and raised six children. They were continuously working on the house, never quite finishing. The exterior was still clad in blue Tyvek insulating material, the porch needed a railing mounted, and some interior rooms were barely framed out. The sound of hammers and drills sounded all weekend as Tim and his oldest children worked on the house.

Tim Jr., the Dawson's oldest and only son, helped unload boxes from the Penske truck. He had a pleasant, shy disposition, and eagerly helped Nick put together the grill, hook up the vent of our dryer to the wall, and assembled Yanni's train set. He helped me unpack, just the bare minimum to make the space more comfortable. The rest of our belongings we piled into the storeroom at the back of the house. The tasks might have provided him some space from his five sisters.

Tessa, whose main preoccupation during the day was to watch her horde of children run around in shorts and bare feet despite the cool summer temperature, was always eager to chat. She clambered from her porch as soon as I appeared below. Wide eyed, I listened as she gave me advice about living in Alaska.

"At the end of the season, the wilting vegetable garden attracts wildlife," she told me. "The moose love my raspberry bushes. One once ventured into the garage when I accidentally left the garage door open."

It took Tim Sr. and Tim Jr.'s hollering and clanking a broom against a metal pipe to send the enormous animal striding, long-legged, out of the garage and into the surrounding woods again. Eager as I was to view the wildlife native to interior Alaska, I told myself I would make sure the garage door stayed firmly shut.

"It's best to take your trash down to the refuse transfer area at the bottom of the hill" Tessa continued importantly, nodding her head for emphasis. "There are no garbage trucks to collect trash out here on the periphery of town."

She paused to holler loudly for her girls who were playing nearby. "And we haul our own water."

When I looked at her blankly, not understanding, she slowed down and spoke to me as though I were a dim-witted child.

"We are not connected to water pipes like folks are in town," she patiently explained. "Tim has a water tank in the bed of his pick-up truck. We have to go fill it once a week at the water station and then fill our reservoir next to the house. The kids keep track of how low the water level is by a gage in the garage." She made a sound halfway between a laugh and a sigh. "But I've had the water run out on me many times anyway."

The younger Dawson girls, smitten with Yanni, played with him. Wearing shorts, bare feet and knees crusted with dirt, they alternated between bumping him around on the gravel of the driveway in his stroller, sometimes climbing in with him to roll, recklessly, down the hill. I sucked in my breath, heart pounding.

In the evening, when the house was quiet, I made a list of all the things I needed to learn first. A grocery store was on the top of the list after I had opened and viewed the contents of the near empty refrigerator. I would have to find the garbage dumpster station that Tessa mentioned to unload the empty packing boxes in the garage. I wanted to stock up on bottled water, just in case. I realized these would be of little help if I happened to be in the shower, hair lathered with shampoo, when the water ran out. I would try to find a clothing store, if there even was a suitable one, so I could buy fleece and boots and hats for the upcoming winter that everyone so far had told me would be formidable and sudden in its arrival.

I studied the map of Alaska that I pinned to the kitchen wall and ran my finger across the names of remote villages, cut off in the wilderness, accessible only by bush planes or by rivers. The names sounded distant, unfamiliar linguistically, a culture removed: Minto, Shishmaref, Galena, Yakutat, Ninilchik, Anaktuvuk Pass, Kachemak, Tuntutuliak. It was as though we had moved to a foreign country.

CHAPTER 5
Max

At the crack of dawn, the first dose of chemotherapy was administered. The pain made it difficult to stay alert. I had to make a concerted effort to answer the questions nurse Ruth was asking.

"You need to tell us the minute you feel funny in any way," she said, frowning. "If you have difficulty breathing, or feel pain, or see swelling or a rash."

I waited, poised, for the effects I had heard about to take hold – nausea, vomiting, weakness. All I could feel was the numbing pain in my body. The pain medications had given only temporary relief. At times, the pain was sharp and pointed. It subsided now and again only to seep back ubiquitously into every muscle, every limb, every bone. It moved from one part of the body to the other, stealing through the terrain it intended to conquer. It enveloped me and I was absorbed within it as though it was a part of me. I had almost grown used to it.

I wanted to close my eyes and sleep, to drift out onto an ocean and not be tethered anymore to the hospital bed. I wanted to float above Ruth and Steven, away from the IV line and the starched bed sheets. And then I sat bolt upright, afraid of this drifting, not allowing it.

The G-CLAC medicines trickled slowly. Ruth and Steven wore protective gowns, masks, gloves and goggles. Conspicuous yellow biohazard signs were imprinted on the clear bags hanging from the IV pole. I thought about the poison that would flow into my body. For my whole life my body had been my friend. I closed my eyes and wished it to be strong, to be able to endure the poison I needed to overwhelm it with. I had to relinquish control. My body needed to do the work now. I was counting on it.

Later that day a chaplain walked into my room.

"I am a non-denominational counselor," she said.

I curled into myself on the bed.

"I am here to offer some words of comfort."

She wore a skirt and an oversized sweater. Clipped onto her sweater were several tags identifying her occupation. Her face was plain and honest, her brown hair tied back sensibly into a barrette. It was evident that talking to me was part of the duties assigned to her. My situation must be dismal if chaplains were already being sent to talk to me. I bristled, wanting her to go, not wishing to talk about my illness. I turned my face to the window.

"Unfortunately, I can't take away your illness," she said, dolefully. "Have you encountered instances of death before?"

I shook my head. All of my immediate family members were still alive. Was she implying that death was the definitive course I was on? I scowled.

"How about Max?" Nick, who was listening from where he sat in the armchair, asked quietly. He must have perceived that I could not bear to talk about myself. Max, our first golden retriever, had passed away suddenly, not quite a year old. We had escaped the Alaskan winter for a few days and were returning from a holiday, overnighting in Miami, when my cell phone vibrated on the hotel room's nightstand. The dog sitter's shrill, panicking voice reached me over the thousands of miles that separated us. She had called several times already to no avail, only reaching voice mail. Something terrible had happened to Max. She returned home to find our dog immobile and lifeless. She did not understand what happened. He was fine when she left the house that morning. Perhaps he ingested something poisonous? The veterinarian examined the dog's body but was unable to find malignancies. The dog was young and, to all perceptions, healthy.

I cried for the entire nine and a half hours it took us to fly back to Alaska. I vowed I would not replace Max. Sometime later, despite scars on our hearts, we found Buddy, another golden retriever. He was the last of his litter. When he arrived from Anchorage in a dog crate, with oversized ears and a twisted corkscrew tail, we realized he was no show dog. Still, we softened at his sight. Max was relegated into a more distant category of beings not forgotten or dismissed, but solemnly commemorated and stowed.

"*Would this be the case with me, too?*" I thought, darkly.

I was angry with the chaplain but envied her faith at the same time. I had not had the time to think about religion, to place the gravity of my situation into a larger, more spiritual context. I did not possess that crutch. Sunday morning church services, praying at meals and talking to God at bedtime were never part of my upbringing. My understanding of the world was orchestrated by my love of nature, its intricacies, its perfect balance. In some rational recess of my mind, I understood the system of nature's checks and balances, of the survival of the fittest. The strong prevailed while the frail were weeded out. My heart wanted to cast aside this balance and logic of the natural world. The theory surely couldn't encompass me as well, could it?

A screaming in my head kept repeating itself: "Why me? Why me?"

Slippery and elusive, the answer fluttered somewhere beyond my grasp. It was like Max's passing: shrouded and beyond explanation. When the chaplain left, I breathed a sigh of relief.

CHAPTER 6
"Midnight Sun"

"I learned today what Alaskans call a 'Sourdough'," Nick exclaimed brightly, bursting into our small kitchen in the Dawson's house after a long day at the clinic.

Since beginning work at the clinic, Nick constantly brought home stories his patients told him. Thus, we learned about the best rivers to fish in. Red salmon were best caught in the Kenai River, standing elbow to elbow in what locals called "combat fishing." Silver salmon were plentiful at Montana Creek. Dip-netting for sockeyes was best in the Copper River where one had to tie oneself to a tree on the steep banks of the river in order to withstand the force of the huge fish getting caught in the handheld nets. Catching a King salmon, in any river, was exhilarating.

We heard about great hiking trails north of Fairbanks, close to the forks of the Chena River. The trails climbed up to heights where wildflowers were dwarfed in the landscape and the vistas were sweeping. We were told about Chena Hot Springs, an hour's drive east, nestled among rolling hills and forests. Its sulfuric water and scent of rotten eggs reached us well before even encountering the rock pool.

I glanced up at Nick from the table, where I was feeding Yanni spaghetti for his dinner. Sourdough? As in blueberry pancakes? Or sourdough bread?

"It's someone who is sour on Alaska but doesn't have the dough to get out!" Nick said in an outburst of laughter.

Yanni, face covered in marinara sauce, cackled at his father. I had to smile as well. I loved the anecdotes. Since I was mostly tied to the apartment and its immediate surroundings because of our young son, the stories provided a welcome extension into life in Alaska. I started a journal where

I recorded first impressions, knowing that time would soon glaze over their novelty.

Summer in Alaska had erupted into a frenzy of activity, almost as though Fairbanksans had to jam into the long days all the outdoor undertakings and proceedings that would stop once winter came. The possibilities of the long evenings seemed endless. People mowed their grass late at night and planted begonias under the midnight sun. Sometimes they even forgot to feed their children dinner. Kayakers and rafters drifted downstream on the slow, brown current of the Chena River which flowed lazily through the town. Around the summer solstice, festivals and fairs were planned. Booths were set up downtown that sold gifts and memorabilia and woodcrafts. Bluegrass bands took to a wooden stage. Food vendors abounded, selling moose burgers and side striped shrimp skewers and fried pickles. A baseball game, known locally as "The Midnight Sun Game" was played without artificial lights, starting at ten in the evening. It attracted a multitude of spectators who erupted into cheers of joy when the sun broke free of the cloud cover close to midnight to shine down upon the final innings.

How could anyone turn sour on Alaska?

For us, that first summer, nothing was cast in a negative light. We absorbed our surroundings like sponges, eager to become part of this new, wild land. Under the birches the forest floor was covered with blue bells and wispy ferns and little red berries. I ventured out on walks, trailed by Yanni who toddled after me, reaching out with pudgy hands for moss covered rocks and small pink wild roses. On some days, the mosquitoes swarmed thick. I covered our heads with mosquito nets, sprayed our clothing with Deet, and swatted away the huge, sluggish insects. It did not deter us from our outings. Even when the smoke of distant wildfires drifted into the town, filling the air with the acrid scent of burned willow and spruce and making our eyes water, we simply ignored it. The winds would pick up sooner or later and drive the smoke out of the valley again.

One weekend Nick joined some colleagues from the clinic for a float trip down the Gulkana, a river swift and wild and clear. With two boats they floated for three days, stopping to fish for rainbow trout and Arctic grayling, and setting up camp along the riverbank at night.

"The canyon was the best," Nick exclaimed, tanned and unshaven and exhilarated. "We went through class four rapids there, in a gorge of churning water."

I was caught halfway between disappointment and gratitude that I had not been there.

The next day, a Saturday, we went on a long bike ride. It was a lesser excursion, but one that Yanni could partake in. Bumping him along in an attached bicycle trailer, we followed the northern outskirts of town on a bike path. It was a mild morning, sun already high, and the scent of wildflowers drifted to us from the fields along the path. We crossed gravel roads named after flowers: Delphinium Lane and Madcap Drive and Fireweed Street. At the end of our ride, on the far end of town, we sat on the banks of the wide Tanana River, watching the silty, glacially fed water flow by.

The Tanana River, a "trail river" as the natives of Interior Alaska called it, had been a transportation route for hundreds of years. I imagined Athabaskans traveling the broad water in birchbark canoes and skin boats. Later, explorers would follow in steamboats and sternwheelers, accommodating for the relatively shallow waters.

Fairbanks existed because of the river. I had read that had it not been for low water on the Tanana River, E.T. Barnette, at the turn of the century, would never have been forced up the Chena River at its confluence with the Tanana. Barnette, seeking to establish a trading post at Tanana Crossing, made a deal with the sternwheeler captain of the *Lavelle Young*. In the event they could not go further upriver due to the shallow water, Barnette and the supplies he needed for the trading post—horses, food, equipment—would simply be left ashore. When the sternwheeler did indeed get stuck in the Chena River, Barnette was left off on a high bank which later developed into the settlement of Fairbanks. It was a tiny post in an immeasurable land. When gold was found not too far north the following year, Fairbanks's future was solidified. Gold prospectors streamed to it, keen on luck and fortune. Fairbanks grew into a larger, identifiable place on a map.

How brave one would have needed to be to establish a home in the wilderness, alone, with no civilization around. For hundreds of miles there were only rolling hills and tight spruce woods and wildlife. And yet I could understand the draw of living on the banks of a river near the flowing water even if the connection to others was remote. It was an undisturbed place. We sat for some time, tired from pedaling, and listened to the drift of the water. We did not want the day to come to an end.

"Let's go to the gold camp for dinner," Nick suggested, as though reading my thoughts.

We sought out the Ester Gold Camp, five miles outside Fairbanks, where we heard we could get a dinner of crab legs and reindeer stew. It was yet another new experience for us. We walked around the site of the original gold mining camp, along with other summer tourists, to explore the bunkhouses of the miners. In a nearby stream, one could still pan for gold. We peeked into the Malamute Saloon where a can-can show transported the audience back to the times of the gold rush.

"Where are you from?" asked a lady from Iowa, part of a large group of tourists a tour bus had just dropped off. She sat down next to us at the long wooden bunkhouse table, dressed in pale blue drawstring shorts and white sneakers, sunglasses perched on the top of her head.

I was not sure how to answer. "We moved to Fairbanks from Ohio," I finally replied. My comment sparked her interest.

"Oh!" she said. "How long have you been here?"

"About three weeks."

"So, you haven't experienced a winter here yet?" she cackled loudly. "Well, that'll probably make you leave again!"

I turned away from her, irritation prickling. I was not sure whether I was more annoyed at her or at myself. She had questioned our move north, pointing out that I was still a newcomer, ignorant of life in the Far North. I had to concede that I still felt like a visitor, partaking enthusiastically in the activities summer offered, but not yet feeling at home.

CHAPTER 7
Alaskan Family

"Is it true my mom has leukemia?" Yanni, just barely eleven, asked Rebecca in a panic. He had called her from the school's office phone. Rumors were circulating before I had even had the chance to speak with my children directly.

Rebecca sighed, resigned and vexed. She had already stepped in far beyond the role of the surrogate parent I forced her to be in.

"I think it's best for you to speak with your parents," she told him gently. "They will be able to explain the details most accurately."

Yanni and Helen were in Fairbanks, fragile and alone. Rebecca and Tara, my friends, took turns caring for their needs. The children's minds must certainly have been racing with frightened thoughts. Neither Nick nor I had even spoken with them since our rushed departure from Alaska.

Over the phone, I tried to keep my voice from shaking when I spoke with Yanni. "It's a disease of the blood. I need to get chemotherapy, a strong medicine for it."

"But you told me it was a pain in your back," he retorted, not understanding.

"That's how the symptoms first presented themselves," I tried to explain. "As a pain in my lower back. But really it's everywhere in my body."

"Because blood flows everywhere in the body?" His young mind was grappling to make sense of it.

"That's right," I told him quietly.

"How long will you be in the hospital?"

"I'm not sure, honey. We'll have to wait and see what the doctors say."

"But they will fix it, right?" His voice sounded small.

"Of course they will," I told him with a confidence I did not feel.

I had never lied to my son before.

Somehow, I managed to divert the conversation to his ice hockey practice, a topic he was always eager to discuss.

"I assisted in three goals yesterday!"

His rushing, excited words belied his young age. My illness registered, but only insofar as it might have an impact on the logistics of his life. For once I felt grateful that he had the sport as an outlet and his teammates for support. At other times, I would have grumbled about the time I spent driving him to and from games and practices at the ice rink in the dark, frigid evenings of the Alaskan winter, time I would much rather have spent reading a book by the fireplace.

I wondered whether Helen, who was only nine, understood the severity of the situation. Her voice came high and clear when her brother handed her the telephone.

"I'm going skiing on Moose Mountain with Roan," she gushed out. "As soon as there's enough snow."

She told me about playing with our new puppy, Buddy, in the raked-up autumn leaves that afternoon. Tara, under the pretext of teaching the energetic dog to properly walk on a leash so that he would not topple me over on my return, took Helen and Buddy on a long walk. I knew that Tara was trying to calm the little girl's fears into a common, constructive purpose.

"Roan and I baked brownies from scratch," Helen prattled on. "And Tara made us hot chocolate."

I was thankful for Helen's nonchalance, her ability to still ignore the fact that the world had changed. Life beyond me continued. My eyes welled up with gratitude and dismay. Helen talked on, about her day at school and homework and puppy training, but soon her voice was a murmur. My thoughts veered.

We needed help. For the first time in our lives, we could not manage alone. The obstacles staggered us. There was Nick's practice to think about. Temporarily closed, monitored by skeletal staff, his employees and patients waited. I could not imagine Nick taking care of their concerns at present. He spent many years training, often spending sleepless nights in the hospital's call room. When he returned home in the morning, gritty eyed and exhausted, he fell into his bed while I tried to keep the children quietly playing. After all his efforts to ameliorate and help others he now found himself on the other end, in his patients' position. Somewhere, in the dimness of my mind, I worried about the financial repercussions. We had medical insurance, of course, but I wondered how much of the treatment would be covered. The medevac flight alone from Fairbanks to Seattle would have been astronomical. Our house stood empty with winter approaching. Tasks needed finishing.

"Who can help us?" I thought, stricken.

Then I brightened. We had already called upon our "Alaskan family" to help. We would take our example from the people native to the land. Alaska's cold and unforgiving environment demanded the cohesion of family for survival. The Athabaskans of Interior Alaska adapted to the long, cold winters and the unforgiving environment by counting on each other for food and shelter. Game and fish were considered community property. Larger kinship groups provided a sense of community. They lived in small, remote villages along great rivers, relying heavily on each other. They hunted and fished during the summer months in order to prepare for the winter. Their resources, whether moose, bear, caribou, salmon or whitefish, sustained the entire village. Men hunted. Women processed not only the food but also the material the hunted animals provided for clothing, baskets, shelters, boats, and snowshoes. Theirs was a symbiotic relationship, at once deeply dependent upon each other yet remarkably independent from the rest of the world.

For us adapted Alaskans, as well, who chose to make ourselves a home in the Far North the need existed to seek out neighbors. Since we lived so far from our real families and travel costs often impeded frequent trips to visit them, we found in our friends and neighbors our own constructed kinship group. They became a substitute extended family. We could call upon each other without question. Sometimes this took the form of simple favors: checking on a friend's house during a cold snap while they were on holiday to ensure the heat was working; waiting in a warm car by a snowy school bus stop to pick up a child whose parent was delayed at work; borrowing eggs or vegetables when supermarket delivery trucks from the Lower 48 States were suspended due to inclement weather and icy road conditions.

Our present circumstance, of course, would demand much more than these neighborly gestures. It would take all of our effort, I slowly realized, to concentrate on my health, to say nothing about the financial backlash of my treatment. The rest of our life—our children, our home, our life as we knew it needed to be given over to whatever persons magnanimous enough to step up to help.

We would work out practicalities with Rebecca and Tara. They were my queen worker bees, circling around my needs. I would ask them to continue caring for the children, to drive them to school and hockey, to take the dog, to watch over the house. No phone call would go unanswered, no missive unnoticed. A wash of relief flooded me.

"…and tomorrow we are going to watch the Nanooks hockey game," Helen's voice heaved me back.

I tried to focus, scrambling for words, reconnecting to the conversation. I had not heard what she was telling me. I felt a sting behind my eyes. I was not there for my little girl.

CHAPTER 8
Induction

"The drugs are so potent that they will destroy many of your healthy cells as well," Ruth warned.

She arrived early in the morning to administer a second dose of chemotherapy. Each session, for the next seven days, would last three hours.

"It's called the induction round," Ruth explained. "We want to get you into remission, to drive the disease into its last recesses, hopefully eradicate it."

She checked my IV line and the port it was connected to. Then she told me about the side effects. Fast dividing cells, such as in the skin and hair, were susceptible. The cells of the digestive tract, from the mouth to the intestines, were particularly vulnerable. I would develop mouth sores, diarrhea, stomach pain. I should be prepared for my hair to fall out. My skin would develop rashes and slough off. Weight loss was inevitable. The list of side effects overwhelmed me. I listened, sickened, stomach clenched tight.

I was glad when Nick took over the conversation. He had spent another night cramped uncomfortably in the armchair by my bed, wanting to be present when Dr. Eakins and his team came into the room on their early morning rounds. When they appeared, the medical students went over the changes that had occurred overnight. My hemoglobin and hematocrit levels had lowered. My white cells were dwindling. This was the intended goal. I hovered on the sideline, half listening.

"This chemotherapy regimen has been successful on patients with similar markers," Dr. Eakins said. He brought out his laptop and showed Nick a medical article referring to such statistics. They looked at the screen for a few minutes.

"Her results could advance further studies and research," Dr. Eakins concluded, looking at me.

I tried to follow their discussion, concentrating on the medical jargon. They spoke technically, then theoretically. I wondered whether they had forgotten I was in the room as well. Perhaps my connection to Nick made them presume I was entrenched in the medical field as well, that I needed less explanation, fewer translations. They spoke of statistics and time frames and the relative value of different medications. Graphs were consulted and numbers were calculated to place me into a spectrum of chances and failures.

I was not thinking of academic trials. I thought only of two young children, alone in Alaska, to whom I needed to return to at all cost. I did not care for drug names and statistics. I wanted to hold my children close again.

After the medical team left the room, Nick sat down next to me and reached for my hand. In his thorough manner he clarified the medical discussion for me.

"The most important thing is to get you into a state of remission. The chemo needs to suppress the cancer. Then we need to make sure it stays that way and doesn't return."

"What are the chances it will return even if I get into remission?" I asked valiantly, though I did not want to hear the answer.

"It's difficult to say," Nick was frank. "The sooner you get into remission, the better. The longer the cancer lingers, the more probable it will return."

"What if I don't go into remission?"

"If you don't go into remission, it's because the cancer cells have found a way to resist the treatment," Nick explained gravely. "It's a little like your body getting used to antibiotics. It doesn't respond anymore if you take them all the time. Cancer cells evolve. They replicate and change. They can resist the agent. But we have other chemo regimens that we can use then."

"What if the cancer cells resist the other medications as well?" I prodded.

Nick sighed.

My mother Inge arrived from Germany on a Wednesday afternoon, four long days after my diagnosis. She came straight from Sea-Tac airport to the hospital. At the door to my hospital room, she dropped her bag and came quickly to me.

"*Ist es sehr schlimm?*" she asked, embracing me, rocking me gently back and forth. *Is it very terrible?*

My tears came suddenly, a torrent, an uncontrollable weeping. I finally nodded, unable to speak past the constriction in my throat. We sat for a long time, she on the edge of my hospital bed, until my sobbing quieted.

A safety net was fastened beneath me. I was not sure whether it would stay taut. For now, however, I felt as though someone had placed their hands beneath me to steady me. I closed my eyes. My mother was nearby. It was the first time I had cried since I had been told about my cancer.

CHAPTER 9
Watershed

Close to the Alaskan summer solstice, mid-June, we hiked onto Angel Rocks. It was deemed an easy hike by locals. The three-and-a-half-mile loop trail first took us along the Chena River's north fork, then through taiga woods, across a mushy tundra boardwalk and finally up a steep incline until it reached the jagged boulders from which the hike took its name.

Our preparations had taken some time. Nick gathered the necessary equipment in the Dawson's garage while I stood alongside. Yanni, perched on my hip, took in the activity with large, unblinking eyes. Backpack, water bottles, mosquito repellent, head nets, bear bells, bear spray, gun. Catching my gaze, Nick grinned.

"At least we don't have to worry about snakes and alligators up here! If a bear is going to eat us, we'll see it coming!" His peal of laughter echoed around the garage. "And if not, it'll just be overkill." He grinned, chuckling at his own pun. I swallowed.

We drove for an hour northwest along Chena Hot Springs road to get to the trailhead. The northern outskirts of town were punctuated with aspen, spruce and birch trees. The two-lane road rose over hills and afforded us, to the south, expansive views of the Tanana Valley and the Alaska Range in the distance. Houses, little more than cabins, were tucked away in the trees. We recognized their existence only by clusters of mailboxes on the road. They became sparser the further we drove.

We passed Two Rivers, a tiny community with scattered houses, a lodge, a church, a school. I noticed dog sled crossing signs and kept my eyes on the trail that ran alongside the road in hopes of catching sight of a dog team and musher. They practiced their runs in the summer as well as winter, I heard, trading the winter sled for a four-wheeler. The wilderness around Two Rivers was crisscrossed with extensive dog mushing trails. Sled dogs outnumbered humans here.

Further down the road the forest was black and burned, ravished by last year's wildfire. The charred remains of dark trunks stood in eerie contrast to the bright blue sky. Fireweed, the first of the flora to re-emerge after a forest fire, pushed its way through the blackened earth again. Its blossoms were not yet visible, but I recognized its elongated leaves from an Alaskan wildflower book. It was a plant obstinate in the aftermath of destruction.

Some miles later, where the road meandered alongside the river, the forest grew thick and green again. We passed trailheads. Granite Tors and Chena Dome and Angel Rocks. We set off along a path next to the glistening, rushing river with Yanni strapped into a toddler backpack. I trudged behind them, soon out of breath as the trail began its steep ascent. Our exertion was worth the effort. When we rounded a corner just below the first craggy boulder, a sweeping vista presented itself. An expanse of mountain ranges fell away in shades of green and azure and purple, as far as we could see. I drew in my breath.

"No wonder they call Alaska the edge of the world," I whispered to myself. It was beautiful and frightening alike.

Protruding massively behind us, competing with the variegated greens of the mountainside, stood the Angel Rocks. They towered above us, one grander than the next. Composed of ancient rock, light colored granite streaked with darker basalt, their tips were exposed through millions of years of erosion. They held stories embedded: silent testimony to the many hikers and wanderers who came to behold them over the years, who then humbly retreated down the trail.

We, too, just newly arrived in this northern land, stood demurely and looked out over the mountains. We could not know what Alaska—beautiful and dangerous and invigorating—held in store for us. We felt its stir in our blood.

We looked down upon the watershed on the distant slopes from the heights of Angel Rocks. The drainage started high near the last snowmelt and meandered among creases. Water parted, losing itself in the mountains, only to find itself again. It trickled towards a valley, a river, a home. Alaska was our own watershed, a twist in our lives, a time of change. Had we made the right decision? A shiver went down my spine as I stood closer to Nick and Yanni. Like so many others, we left behind a familiar and predictable life in Ohio to pursue the adventure that was Alaska, in search of gold or oil or fur, like the prospectors and adventurers and dreamers before us. Living in the bush, many of them had failed and fled.

I turned to look at the ancient boulders behind me. We were among rocks. As well as angels.

CHAPTER 10
Dwindling Counts

"We need to make sure you don't develop a neutropenic fever," Dr. Eakins told me.

He stopped by to check on me without his medical entourage, dressed in street clothes—sweater, button down shirt, khaki pants—rather than his usual scrubs. To me, this was more alarming than comforting. Was the trial drug regimen not progressing favorably enough that he would feel the need to come in on his day off?

He looked at me over the top of his bifocals as he read the last note in my chart. "An infection in high-risk patients like yourself, at a time when you have virtually no white blood cells to counteract it, would be detrimental."

Ruth and Steven recorded my "counts" into the chart daily. In a steady downward trend, my red and white cells dwindled, leaving me anemic because of the former and highly susceptible to infections because of the latter. Because my immune system was so compromised, the nurses took great measures to safeguard the environment I lived in. Masks and gowns were worn by all entering the room. Visitors with respiratory ailments were banned from the hospital floor altogether. All surfaces were painstakingly cleaned with strong germicidal wipes. Hand sanitizers were strategically placed. A special meal plan for "immunosuppressed" patients was sent up to my room every day, food that I left mostly untouched.

"What kinds of infections?" I asked Dr. Eakins, not because I wanted to really know but because Nick, who generally asked the medical questions for me, had gone to use the restroom at the end of the hallway.

"Pneumonia, cellulitis, intra-abdominal sepsis, lung infiltrates," Dr. Eakins' voice trailed off. He was focused again on my chart. When he lowered his head to study the laptop, I noticed that he had carefully combed strands of thinning hair over a bald spot on the top of his head.

After he left, I called Tara in Alaska.

"It's a fever called neutropenia. It sounds like a shampoo, doesn't it?" I said, trying to make the ominous sound lighthearted.

Tara, always ready to banter, agreed. She then turned the conversation to Maria, Nick's sister, in Fairbanks. She had come from Greece to help take care of the children and to alleviate the burden on my friends.

"She doesn't want to drive either in the snow or in the dark," Tara laughed. "That more or less eliminates Alaska. Rebecca and I have to drive up to your house twenty times a day. There is always something she needs."

I pictured Maria, nine years Nick's senior. In Greece, she was the seamless orchestrator of her home, the stronghold of her family, the glue that held the clan together. Unruffled, she could put together meals to serve a party of ten in a matter of no time, heartily serving platters of lamb and lemon potatoes and *moussaka* to those gathered around her dining table. When asked to fly to Fairbanks, however, to sort out her passport and pack a bag, she moaned and resisted. The flight was too long, her health was not good, Alaska was so cold. She did not trust herself to drive on the snowy roads. She felt unsure about staying alone in the house at night, with only the children for company.

Tara cackled on the other end of the line.

"Yesterday the kids went to their friends' for a sleepover. Maria was by herself and asked me to come over and spend the night with her. I told her, no offense, Maria, but you are no Leonardo di Caprio!"

Just then Ruth walked into the room, putting an end to our jesting on the telephone. "Let's go for a walk," she encouraged. "It is important for you to move so that your muscles do not atrophy."

I hung up the phone, drawn back to my hospital room reality. I reluctantly heaved myself to the side of the bed. The unyielding pain surged again. I walked the length of the corridor, pushing the IV pole that was attached to me, my gait slow and arduous. At the nurse's station, I encountered Nick, returning from the restroom. I was glad to have his arm to hold onto.

The hallways were connected in a triangle. A marathon's length. At its apex, double doors led out to the elevators and the rest of the hospital. Signs warned of the sensitive hospital floor environment and warded off visitors with respiratory illnesses. I peered through the doors at the world outside, off limits to me now. We doubled back to my room. I sat down on my bed, thankful to not crumple into myself. Nick and Ruth exchanged a glance as they helped me lift my legs back up on the bed.

I was rapidly deteriorating. I saw it in their faces. It was evident in my body that had lost over thirty pounds very quickly.

Ruth handed me the water bottle on my tray table and arranged the sheets over my legs. I sipped with difficulty, the water dribbling down my chin. I touched my fingers to my lower lip and chin. They felt numb, like the sensation of a dentist's anesthetic that would not wear off.

Once again, I was wheeled through the labyrinthine hallways of the hospital's basement, where the radiology department was housed. The leukemia caused infiltrates, clumps of diseased cells that permeated stealthily and dangerously into my body's tissue in different areas. They were damaging nerves and taking over. Even though my lower face was affected, the ultrasound ordered this time was of my liver. I was confused. Perhaps my blood test results revealed something else to prompt this scan.

The radiology technician scanned the ultrasound monitor with her eyes, searching my liver for signs of damaged cells. I concentrated on her neutral expression which she masked for my benefit. Did I see a moment's hesitation in her gaze as she scanned the computer? Was that the semblance of a frown? I thought about the other times in my life that I had an ultrasound performed on me. I was pregnant then, expecting Yanni and Helen. On those occasions the indistinct, grainy, monochromatic sonograms promised the thrill of our future. They had enveloped me with excitement for what was to come. The world was in order then.

Returning to my room, my stomach knotted up. I locked myself into the bathroom. A separate space, some distance. Steven had placed "hats" into the toilet in order to monitor my bowel movements. Constipated and bloated, I was unable to deliver and sat, hunched over myself, on the cold metal bench in the bathroom's shower instead. My legs had shrunk to half of their size. My bony knees were larger than my thighs. I stared at them aghast.

I could die. I broke out into a cold sweat. I clasped my hands together to keep them from trembling and felt the surge of bile in my throat. I was standing on a precipice. A canyon gorge, large and deep, opened up beneath me. There was no foothold I could place my trembling foot upon. I understood now why Nick gently suggested, in hushed tones earlier that day, that I have a talk with Yanni and Helen. Perhaps it was best to explain the circumstances to them clearly. Wheezing, I had to remind myself to breathe. Perhaps he was right. But how would I find the appropriate words to tell them that my chances of survival were slim? And how could they possibly continue living life for me, after I was gone?

Hot tears streamed down my face. I wanted to scream but just an asphyxiated, strangled sound emerged from my throat. I was indignant with Nick, for having seen so many diseases and outcomes throughout his medical career that he told me we must brace ourselves for the worst. I was angry at my mother for taking an ostrich approach, wanting to put her head in the sand at a time of danger. "Let's take this day by day," she said, placing her hand on my arm. She, too, did not want to hear that my prognosis was poor. I was incensed at Dr. Eakins, for his detached interest in my disease as a statistic and a formula for the future. Most of all I was irate at myself for getting sick. My instinct as the mother of my children was to deflect from danger, to comfort, to make the world well again.

It was late when I finally let myself out of the bathroom again. I called Rebecca, desperate for the sound of a friend. I could not manage my voice very well.

"I'm trying to do this with any amount of grace I can gather," I told her, miserably. "I don't know how I should tell the kids."

There was a pause before she calmly answered.

"You don't need to tell them anything. Because everything you need to tell them you already have."

My tears subsided a little. I felt just the tiniest lifting of the weight in my heart.

CHAPTER 11
Prisoner of Darkness

My children stood by my hospital bed, wearing oversized yellow gowns and facemasks to protect me from contaminants. Their rushing words tumbled into each other.

"They gave us Digi players on the flight," Helen was kindled by excitement. "We watched *Gnomeo and Juliet*."

"I had to sit next to a huge man," Yanni complained, though his face wore a grin. "I couldn't even get by him to go to the bathroom."

"The flight attendant gave us a sandwich," Helen said. "But mine had pesto on it so I didn't want it. Yanni ate it."

"It took *forever* to get here from the airport," Yanni commented. "There were so many cars on the highway. Seattle is huge."

My pain was temporarily blotted out as I listened to their jabber. The children had flown from Fairbanks to Seattle by themselves for the weekend. Nick collected them at the airport and brought them to the hospital, where my mother and I waited in anticipation. My mother had not seen her Alaskan grandchildren in many months. For me, the week since I had left them behind in Fairbanks seemed like an eternity.

We talked, interrupted once by Steven who came to take my temperature and check my blood pressure. Yanni and Helen took in his proceedings, following his moves with big eyes. Steven smiled at them before he left the room again. When Nick saw my energy dwindle, he shepherded them to the hospital cafeteria for lunch. I glowered. Even the simple act of listening to my children exhausted me.

In the afternoon, feeling a little more rested, I went for a corridor walk with Helen and Yanni.

"Why do you have to have the IV pole with you all the time," Helen asked, watching me arrange the tubing so I wouldn't step on it as I got out of bed.

"The medicines take a long time to flow through," I explained. "This way I don't have to stay in bed the whole time and we can go for a walk."

Satisfied, Helen offered to navigate my IV pole, rolling it alongside as we made slow progress down the corridor. I winced at the pain in my legs but smiled at her, camouflaging the effort it took to walk the simple length of a hallway. Yanni, who had walked ahead of us, stood by a hallway window. His attention was on the University's Husky Stadium below. The outdated football stadium was being renovated. The south side of the stadium was already demolished. Cracked concrete, torn-apart bleachers and mounds of crumbled walls filled the site. Dump trucks, heavy machinery, orange fencing and workers in hard hats populated the construction zone. Any concern for my condition was instantly replaced by this new interest. We stood at the window for a while watching the activity below before we resumed our cumbersome walk back to my room.

That evening, after my family left for the hotel, I could not rest. The hospital floor was quiet. The familiar daytime sounds of voices, beeping monitors and the squeak of rolling gurneys was absent. My room was dark, except for the nightlight that the nurse left on for me, which cast an eerie glow onto the wall.

I was filled with thoughts of death. I was careening towards it. We all knew this implicitly. Death's possibility, when I had so much more to do with my life, clutched me with dismay. My children were young and dependent. My husband needed my support. The plans we had envisioned for our future had not yet materialized. There was so much I still needed to do.

I realized what I was up against. I was coping with the odds. I was alone. No one could help, much as they wanted to. I was in this by myself. Everyone on shore was reaching out to me as I was being carried away on a current, but no one could firmly grasp my outstretched hand. It was futile. I thought of obituaries in newspapers, describing someone's peaceful passing, with family gathered around the bedside. It seemed ludicrous to me. One dies alone. Sometime in the early hours of the morning, I finally fell into an exhausted sleep.

When morning came and the children were again with me, I breathed a little easier. We went on our walk. The children noticed a police officer sitting on a metal folding chair outside a patient's room at the end of the hallway. Curiosity immediately aroused, they looked unabashedly through the open doorway. Both gasped when they caught sight of the patient. His foot was shackled to the bedpost.

"There's a *prisoner* down at the end of the hallway," Yanni spilled out to Nick upon returning to my room. "A policeman is guarding his door!"

Nick, who had seen a multitude of patients over the course of his training, put down the article he was reading and pulled him closer.

"In a large hospital like this one there are all sorts of patients," he explained. "Even convicts need to be treated for their medical conditions, regardless of the crimes they may have committed."

Yanni's imagination took hold. "But what if he's a murderer?"

Nick quietly answered, "It is still our duty as doctors to heal people, if we can."

I listened. Compared to the convict's outlook of returning to prison after his treatment, perhaps my destiny, whatever its course, did not look quite so bleak. I, at least, could count the number of days we had all spent on this earth together as a family, a team of four. I was glad that I didn't know how many days we would still have together. I wanted to cherish the overlap of days granted to us. Each day further with them was reason enough to keep going. What family, if any, did the prisoner have?

When the weekend came to an end, a dark, empty ache settled within me.

"We'll see you at home soon, Mom," Yanni told me, determined.

The semblance of a smile crossed his face. I nodded bravely. A lump solidified in my throat. Helen embraced me fiercely, in the manner she used to when she was very little, crushing against me. Her eyes filled slowly, lower lip trembling. When Nick gently disentangled her clutch around my neck, I reigned in my emotion and smiled at her.

"Take good care of Buddy," I instructed.

After they left, I laboriously got out of my bed and walked down the hallway to its very end. I could see the broad water that was Lake

Washington and the bridge across to Bellevue. The mountains rose in the far distance. Beyond those mountains my children would fly and with each passing mile we would be further apart. My back slid down the hallway wall until I sat in a shapeless heap on the hospital tiles. My shoulders heaved and the tears that I had valiantly fought off while the children were with me silently trailed down my face. Incarcerated, I was as much a prisoner of my body as of my mind.

CHAPTER 12

Homestead

"Don't think for a minute this place is anything like the States," Traci, the realtor, laughed. "There's a little bit of everything up here."

I sat next to her, bumping along the gravel roads in her huge Yukon SUV, through what she, chuckling, had called "the suburbs" of Fairbanks. She was a large woman with an infectious laugh. Her cell phone, which she kept tucked into her bra and which she retrieved dexterously while negotiating the hilly roads, rang constantly. Hanging up with yet another client, Traci told me that she herself had come to Alaska many years ago from California.

"Believe me, it took some time to get used to the difference," she said. "Housing here can mean all sorts of things."

Traci waved towards the hills rising on our right. "People live up on the Chena Ridge, or above Farmer's Loop Road, but then you have to deal with steep, icy driveways in the winter. In town, the houses are closer together, less expensive. But you have to live with the ice fog that settles in the valley. Some folks live in North Pole, about a twenty-minute drive from here, where real estate is cheaper. It's always colder there than in Fairbanks. Way colder! And then there's any number of dry cabins all over town, but I'm not sure you want to live without running water."

I wasn't sure either. The Dawson's apartment had suited us well up until now. As our first summer was drawing to a close, though, we began casting out for a place of our own. I learned, just a week or two earlier, that I was expecting a baby again. Dazed, I looked at the plus sign take form on the pregnancy test, understanding that we had not taken any measures to prevent this outcome yet astonished at its expedited reality.

When I delivered the news to Nick, he gave me a smile that reached his eyes.

"I'd say it's time we find ourselves a house to call home," he said.

Traci and I drove around all morning, stopping at a drive-through coffee house for a Chai tea to keep the momentum going and my interest engaged. I gazed out at the dwellings we passed. Architecturally, most were sorely lacking in aesthetics. Plain looking, they often resembled oversized garages or functional barracks. In town, the wooden houses were crammed next to each other, as though collectively bracing themselves for the next winter. On the outskirts of town, rustic cabins peered out of the woods with propane tanks and outhouses nearby. We passed nice-looking log houses set back in spacious yards. A little further we saw a series of empty lots resembling junk yards. Bits of rusty equipment—a broken car, an old dishwasher, tarp covered bits and pieces—lay partially hidden among the trees. The cost of removing them was evidently not worth the effort. In Goldstream Valley the houses were scattered farther apart, tucked into wooded lots. On smaller dirt roads there were shacks affixed with huge satellite dishes and conspicuous "No Trespassing" signs.

"And then there's the danger of homes built on permafrost," Traci continued her explanations, pointing to a house on the edge of a field punctuated with stunted black spruce. The trees were unable to find root in the permanently frozen soil beneath them. The house tilted at a slant on the unstable, shifting ground.

I listened, overwhelmed. Finding a house was not going to be an easy task. This town lacked the order and regularity of suburban neighborhoods in Ohio. I wondered whether there existed any housing covenants, regular property owner meetings, efficient infrastructure.

Traci pulled over onto a side street.

"Crap!" she complained as she squinted out of her window. "The worst part about being a realtor in Alaska is that you have to change signs out in the summer. In the winter, I can never read the street signs because of the snow drifts."

She had loaded the trunk of the Yukon with "For Sale" signs. Every so often she stopped in a driveway, hauled out a sign, and hammered it to the nearest birch tree. I wondered at the turnover of houses. Why had their owners left?

When she dropped me at the Dawson's house in the late afternoon, Traci assessed my demeanor.

"Don't worry. We'll find you something," she grinned. "You know what they say about people that move here, right? They either leave after the first winter, hightailing it out of here, or they stay a lifetime." Her laughter followed me indoors.

In the living room, Nick and Yanni were playing with a wooden train. With a sigh, I shrugged off my shoes and went to sit on the carpet next to them.

"I don't know," I answered in response to Nick's raised eyebrow. "There are all sorts of homes up here. I'm not sure of any of it."

Nick turned his attention back to the train, watched Yanni scoot alongside on his bottom as he pushed the locomotive along the track.

"Be patient" he said, maddeningly unconcerned, and imitated the sound of the chugging train.

I went back to the kitchen table, where I had spread out a map of the town. I located the neighborhoods Traci told me about and tried to identify schools. Perhaps I should give it a rest, like Nick suggested, let some time pass before my next outing to look for the right home. I was steeped in it, though, wanting a conclusion. I was still caught in a transitory place, unsettled, uprooted. Perhaps having a house of our own would make Alaska our home.

I turned my attention to an upcoming trip to Germany for my sister's wedding in September. I still needed to sort out a dress to wear, book a flight to Munich and memorize the reading she had asked me to recite at the church ceremony. The wedding date was set long ago. Andrea had planned and prepared for months, deciding on a chapel, sending out invitations, arranging a reception dinner at the *Gasthof*. I folded up the map and put away my jotted down notes. I would return to the project of finding a house later.

I caught a flight to Germany a week later, together with Yanni, bidding Nick a hasty goodbye. He would follow in a few days' time. We were going early to help with the preparatory arrangements, to place final touches on table arrangements, and make appointments with the hairdresser. Just as we were in the midst of wedding preliminaries, looking forward to the upcoming celebration, we were assailed with horrific news. Hijackers had crashed airplanes into the World Trade Center in New York, killing hundreds and leaving the world gasping in front of their television screens. Nick was on the telephone moments later. All air traffic in America had been grounded. He would not be coming to join us.

We proceeded with a wedding subdued because of the appalling attack. With a diminished guest list, we placed the world's problems out of mind temporarily as we watched Andrea and Klaus marry in a small church ceremony and dance their newlywed waltz upon the wooden floorboards of the *Alter Wirt*. When air traffic resumed, I returned to Alaska, desperate to be together with Nick in the face of the horror that had transpired.

Alaska was firmly settled into autumn upon our return. The air turned crisp. The fireweed blossomed up their stalks, turning silvery at their tips, an indication that snow was just six weeks away. Trumpeter swans, arctic loons, and northern shovelers were slowly readying themselves for their migration, soon to fly south in noisy departures. In the White Mountains moose hunting season had begun. Hunters, dressed in camouflage, with guns strapped onto four-wheelers and campers parked on the gravel bars of Quartz Creek, spent days scoping the mountains and trails for moose. Earlier and earlier, the shadows of the evening crept up the orange hillsides.

"Let's drive down to the Park," I suggested to Nick. I did not want to stay in the rented apartment. The allure of the fall colors beckoned. We left my suitcase half unpacked and piled into the car to drive south.

In the rust-colored mountains of Denali State Park, the willow bushes had turned amber. Arctic hares scampered, their paws and ears already turning white in their winter transition. We left the car at a pull-out near Little Coal Creek, pulled on hiking boots and, with Yanni crowing delightedly on Nick's back, started up the trail. The dense forest soon gave way to open tundra as we climbed. Above the tree line, lichen-covered rocks along the trail had turned white. The mountains around us were carpeted in crimson and orange. We could smell the fermenting high bush cranberries. Above us, in a sky blue and expansive, a few puffy cumulus clouds dissipated in the distance.

We came upon a slanting alpine meadow where blueberries spread abundantly. Stopping to catch our breath, Nick unstrapped Yanni from his back and set him down on the spongy tundra where he could reach for the small, tart blueberries surrounding him. The vista swept far through the valley across the braided Chulitna River. Mount Foraker, the Eldridge Glacier and Denali presented themselves to us in full majesty. I inhaled and felt for Nick's hand as he also took in the view.

We hiked to the Kesugi Ridge, the "base of the ancient one," as the Athabaskans called it. For generations they hunted for bear and caribou on land they called their own. They established their hearth in this vast wilderness, an unbound terrain, a land marginally connected. Tightly woven, held together by lineage and descent, they counted on their kinship to anchor themselves even in their semi-nomadic existence.

I felt myself ease as I gazed across the landscape. It did not matter that we did not have a house to call our own. If Andrea and Klaus could start their home in the face of a world grappling with adversity and destruction, we would also overcome the minor obstacles of unsightly dwellings and untidy neighborhoods. It was not about the structure, whether of log or brick, up on a ridge or in a valley, that was important. We could even acquire a piece of land and build ourselves a house. It was all possible, even if we did not have a plan yet. The suggestion of another life was growing within me. Alaska would become our home. Of this I was suddenly certain.

CHAPTER 13
The Factory

The receptionist drew large, yellow, highlighted circles on the clipboard, tapping lacquered fingernails on them in emphasis.

"What is your date of birth? Do you have a port? Have you fallen since your last visit?"

I nicknamed the Seattle Cancer Care Alliance Clinic "The Factory." The waiting room on the first floor teemed with people. A long registration desk, lined with five or six receptionists, was the first stop on the assembly line. Patients were called up. The initial questions were always the same, day after day. I could recite them from memory.

My mother and I sat and waited. I looked at the other patients, judging how much worse they looked than I did. I tried to guess what kind of cancer they had and whether their disease was in remission.

"Does that woman look worse than me?" I whispered to my mother, nudging in the direction of a middle-aged patient, slumped over herself, white skinned and thin. Before she could answer, I nodded towards another patient, a man clutching a walker, shuffling awkwardly towards the reception desk. "Or him?"

They didn't look like they would be going home anytime soon. I eyed the patients around me, measuring myself up against them. I did not assess them, as I might have in the past, as being thinner or taller or blonder than me. I now scrutinized them through cancer's vocabulary: less mobile, more bruised, paler, weaker.

A woman limped in then, with a complexion bruised purple and black, eyes half closed. A hush crossed the waiting room, followed by embarrassed silence and gazes turned down towards magazines. She sat down next to me. For a moment, I wanted to say something to ease her, to include her burden with the rest of us. I halted. It seemed to me that I was further along than she was in my treatment. I looked healthy by comparison. Statistically, if she died, my chances of returning home would be greater. Feeling neither shame nor guilt, I leaned back into my chair. I said nothing.

After my discharge from the hospital, my mother and Nick and I moved into the Seattle Cancer Care Alliance House on Pontius Avenue. The modern, six story structure, with a brown façade and large windows, offered a view of Seattle's downtown skyline. The house was new, the apartment clean. Nevertheless, Nick and my mother immediately started wiping down every surface of the apartment – furniture, windowsills, telephone, closets – with disinfecting Clorox wipes and floor cleansers they bought at a nearby Safeway.

"We need to be extremely careful now," Nick announced in a stern, doctor voice. "To safeguard Birgit from every possible infection."

I sat at the table, watching their progress. Soon the apartment smelled like a chlorinated swimming pool. Even though I had been discharged from the hospital, my counts were still far too low for me to be in any public space, much less board an airplane. The risk of infection was high. My mother and I would remain in Seattle while Nick returned to Alaska on his own.

Nick's concern was evident in his lengthy instructions.

"You must wash your hands every twenty minutes," he said as he watched my mother organize my freshly washed clothing—pajamas, underwear, sweatshirts—into neat piles in the closet. "And stay away from people as much as possible. Their clothes could harbor contaminants and their breathing bacteria."

He stocked the pantry with cans of chicken soup, Ensure supplements and Gatorade. He placed dozens of TV dinners into the freezer.

"Be sure to wipe down all food containers with bleach before opening them. It is best if you only eat cooked food. If you buy fresh fruit and vegetables, you'll need to wash them scrupulously before eating them. Don't take any chances!"

He watched my mother spread a bedsheet over my bed.

"Bed sheets, towels and clothing need to be washed with bleach every single day."

Reluctantly, Nick took his leave the next morning. The demands of his medical practice pressed. The children needed a parent home again.

"You'll be alright here while I'm gone?" he asked, almost as though to convince himself. "I'll be back in a week."

I gave him a smile that quickly dissolved at its corners. "The faster you leave, the faster you'll return," I answered bravely, my courage faltering already. Deflated, I watched him go.

Without him, my uncertainty stretched endlessly in every direction. I wandered, listless and unhappy, through the house. It was a sterilized environment for recuperating cancer patients. Even though it tried to recreate the feel of a communal college living atmosphere, nothing could change the fact that it was a house for the sick. In the enormous communal kitchen, above several cooking "stations," detailed instructions for sterilizing pots and pans after use hung on the wall. Next to high temperature dishwashers, a large pantry was stocked with donated canned foods willingly left behind by patients fortunate enough to have returned home. In the second story living room, comfortable couches and puzzle-laden tables overlooked the high-rise buildings of downtown Seattle. There was a small library, lined with books that had circulated through many hands, pamphlets describing every conceivable cancer. I came across a fitness room, complete with yoga mats and stationary bicycles and wondered whether it existed more for the benefit of caretakers than cancer patients. On the bottom floor, washers and dryers rumbled comfortingly.

Returning to the apartment, I scowled at my mother like an ill-tempered child when she offered me some chicken soup. I sat staring stonily out of the window for the rest of the afternoon.

"Briget…Beerget…Burgit"

A nurse near the reception desk bellowed out mispronounced versions of my name. I had long gotten used to the variations of the German name. I smiled despite my foul mood.

"What an interesting name," the nurse exclaimed, smiling brightly.

"Where are you from? How long have you lived in America? When did you move to Alaska? How is it you don't have much of a German accent?"

Next step in the assembly line: the laboratory.

Rows of blood drawing cubicles, curtained for privacy, lined the room, looking much like a production line. Patients were chuted in and out of these, systematically, replaced one after the other as soon as a cubicle emptied. The smell of Heparin and alcohol hung in the air. Fluorescent lights glared from the ceiling. I sat in front of the drawing table while a nurse arranged tubes on a metal tray. The first order was to clean the Hickman port in my chest. Next, blood was drawn to fill a multitude of tubes with different colored caps. Finally, Heparin was flushed through my port, leaving me with an odd, cold sensation in my chest. I was then told to go up to the fifth floor waiting room to await the lab results and to be assigned to a transfusion room.

My mother and I sat in reclining armchairs. The windows in front of us overlooked Lake Union on which floatplanes took off and landed in the placid water. I longed for Alaska as I watched the small aircraft power up, churning up the water, and glide off smoothly before they took to the air on the far end of the lake near Gas Works Park. In Alaska, every other person had a pilot's license it seemed. The skies above Fairbanks teemed with small airplanes, on their way to fishing and hunting expeditions, on flightseeing trips to the Brooks Range and the Arctic Circle, and on deliveries to bush communities. For someone who had always disliked airplanes, my desire to board one to fly north was suddenly urgent.

Doctors came into the waiting room at intervals, sitting down earnestly next to waiting patients to speak to them in hushed tones. My mother discreetly gazed down at the book she had brought along. I, on the other hand, craned my neck to listen.

"I have small cell lung cancer," an older gentleman told me when he noticed my interest. Flustered, I turned red. When he continued talking, I realized that he really wanted to share his story with me. "It's the worst one to get. There is nothing the medical team can do for me now. It has spread to my bones."

I marveled at his composure. He seemed almost tranquil to me, in the aftermath of a surrendered fight, in an acceptance of fate.

A group of women, all younger than me, huddled together in the corner of the waiting room. They shared a sense of camaraderie and even joked as they compared the sizes of their shrinking breast tumors.

"Sonya laughed her way through chemotherapy," one of them told me, nodding at her friend.

I shook my head, unable to understand this willingness of theirs to embrace their circumstances, to abide by a life dominated by disease. All of them, in their varying stages, did not seem to question their disease's cohabitation in their bodies. It had become a part of them. They would live with it, fighting when possible, only resigning when necessary.

I, on the other hand, bristled and resisted. I needed to go home, quickly flee. I could not become part of this group of patients at the clinic, a piece of cog rail on the assembly line, another patient on the conveyer belt towards relinquishment.

Zzzp, zzzp, zzzp.

The pager I held in my hand vibrated. It was not a pager summoning me to a softly lit restaurant, amid plates of deliciously smelling food, to sit across the table from my husband. Instead, I was being directed to a transfusion room to receive further medical treatment.

I proceeded to my assigned room. The transfusion rooms lining the hallway were numbered and plentiful. Each room contained a bed, a reclining armchair and a side table with a computer on it. There were magazines and extra pillows and water bottles. On the computer screen an image of the SCCA Clinic slowly bounced back and forth. Most rooms were occupied. Patients sat, attached to IV lines securely taped to their chests or arms. Plastic bags hung suspended above them. Nurses pumped up blood pressure cuffs. Doctors reviewed medical orders on the computer. The floor buzzed: a hive of medical industry.

My mother stopped at the kitchenette halfway down the hallway. The refrigerator was stocked with juices and soft drinks; the cupboards with soups and chips and granola bars. My mother picked up a strawberry yoghurt for me. In the infusion room, she helped me onto the bed, propping a pillow behind my back. I maneuvered the incline of the bed to a more comfortable slant.

A serious, no-nonsense nurse dressed in Mickey Mouse scrubs entered. Looking at me over her bifocals, she read off my demographic information from her clipboard to assure herself that the red blood cell transfusion bag she held in her hands was, indeed, the one intended for me. Without sparing a moment for small talk, she hung the bag onto the IV pole next to another bag with straw-colored platelets. She then turned to prepare a G-CSF injection, needle and vial on a metal tray. It was meant to boost my bone marrow into making white blood cells. I winced in anticipation, readying myself for the deep bone pain that I knew would develop shortly after. I was not sure anymore whether the pain, savage and deep in my body, was due to the leukemia or the remedies taken to counteract it. She rubbed an alcohol swab onto my thigh.

"Ready?" She stuck me without waiting for my answer.

"Let me know when the red blood cells are through," she said, pressing a call button into my hand and dialing open the plastic tubing to let the red liquid trickle down. "Then we'll start the platelets." Then she was gone.

My mother and I sat for the next four or five hours until the drip of the bags tapered off. Rain pelted at the windowpane. I drew my blanket around me and listened to the soporific sound of the transfusion machine's pump.

Later that evening we rode the shuttle van along Eastlake Avenue to the SCCA House, bumping along, jostling painfully. I felt drained. With a final herculean effort, I took the elevator to our apartment and collapsed onto my bed. I could not eat, even though my mother offered me some vanilla pudding. She sighed, then drew the bedcover up over my legs. Settling herself at the dining table, in the half-light, she typed a group email to my siblings—Thomas, Michael and Andrea—in Germany:

> *Ihr Lieben.* My dears. Today was another blood transfusion. The injections that are meant to stimulate the growth of white cells seem to cause severe muscle pain. Birgit is very tired. It is hard and painful, but she is bearing the therapy with patience. Nick has left and we are on our own for the week.

I turned and watched her from across the room. She would be inquiring about my father's health. I knew she worried about him even though Andrea reassured her that he was recuperating, albeit slowly, after his own colon surgery. Andrea was doing her best to keep him comfortable in her home. My mother's account to my siblings would be prudent and guarded, as I lay brittle and infirm beside her. Before she turned off the computer for the night, she promised to call the next day to speak with my father.

"You must feel torn between the two of us, both of us needing you," I said to her.

My mother looked at me, sadly.

"*Du bist jetzt wichtiger,*" she replied. *You are more important now.*

She retired to her own bed in the alcove. There she would listen for my breathing to fall into the rhythm of sleep before she could succumb to her own dread of what was happening to her child. I remained awake. How did one, when pressed, choose between a husband and a child?

Years ago, when Nick and I were studying at Oberlin College, we both took philosophy courses. Mine was a survey course, running the gamut of prominent Western thinkers. Nick's was on the philosophy of ethics, probing deeper into the thoughts of Immanuel Kant. Over dinner in Dascomb Hall, Nick told me how his class had discussed the veil of ignorance that Kant had proposed should shroud all ethical decisions.

"If you were in a situation where you could save either a total stranger or your spouse from drowning," Nick described the scenario from class, "whom would you try to save?"

To me, the answer seemed obvious.

Kant would say that you make a rational decision based on your distance from the drowning person and the likelihood that you could actually save them rather than emotionally plunging in headfirst to save your spouse. Personal biases should be minimized, the philosopher wrote. Actions should benefit the goals of society rather than furthering one's own purposes. A veil should be cast so our actions would not be influenced by our personal inclinations. Therefore, instead of futilely jumping into the water to reach a spouse out of reach, one should perhaps try to save the stranger within an arm's span.

I asked myself whether this was even possible. I thought about it until well into the night. My father and I were both drowning. I ached for my mother. A nagging thought settled itself within me. Perhaps I, too, needed to discard the veil of ignorance I had shrouded myself in. I needed to stop resisting my cancer, emotionally flaying my arms and sputtering against it as though it did not exist. Maybe I was exactly like the other cancer patients at the clinic, one of many in the cancer factory, who had to accept what was happening to them. I might not be the one spared and rescued from the water. It could be a total stranger that survived, not me.

CHAPTER 14
Bad Hair Day

It was Rebecca's suggestion.

"Why don't we bring in a hairdresser to shave your head," she gently asked. "It would be better than to watch your hair fall out bit by bit, prolonging the sense of loss, don't you think?"

She had travelled to Seattle with our friend Heather for the weekend. She claimed it was a business trip but more likely they both needed to confirm in person what had happened to me in the past three weeks.

We were sitting around the kitchen table—Rebecca, Heather, my mother and I—with cups of Darjeeling tea in front of us, as though we had gathered for a book club or a game of cards. I had taken a shower just before, to the extent that my energy level allowed, and sat, catching my breath. Rebecca picked up my hairbrush and drew it through my hair. Wisps, then clumps, of hair were left tangled in the bristles and in her hand. She traded a look with my mother and Heather.

The nurses, Ruth and Steven, warned me of this. Still, I was unprepared when it happened. I stared at the hair. Wait! Not yet. I'm not ready. I thought it would fall out all at once, overnight, in the forgiving gesture Rebecca now proposed.

"We could call for a hairdresser to come here. That way, you wouldn't even need to go out."

"No!" I retorted vehemently.

Silence grabbed all of us.

"Why don't we go out for a little?" one of them suggested some moments later, while I tried to lengthen my breathing. Perhaps they sensed my need for time alone. The pretext of an excursion into town, for my mother's sake, who was in Seattle for the first time, seemed plausible. I barely looked up as they left the apartment.

I sat, rankling, in the armchair by the window. Through half-raised blinds, I watched as the people of Seattle went about their day, a world on course while mine had come to a screeching halt. Young professionals, dressed in slacks and heels, sporting umbrellas and smart phones, passed on the sidewalk on their way to nearby Microsoft or Amazon offices. This was not a neighborhood of families, of strollers and school buses and noisy children playing in suburban cul-de-sacs. It was a world with a purpose, confident in youth, aspiring towards a future. People were caught up in the energetic pace of their urban landscape, in a city of sturdy concrete and shiny metal and resplendent windows.

During a sun break in the rainy day, they paused to sit on benches outside Whole Foods with containers of ethnic food for lunch. After work they gathered for Happy Hour at the Lunchbox Laboratory or O'Maille's Irish pub. They talked about work and the boss that had asked for yet another report and the coffee maker in the break room that always malfunctioned. Animated, they planned excursions for the weekends: hiking at Snoqualmie Pass or kayaking along the shores of Puget Sound. When they returned to their parked cars, with a vista of distant Mount Rainier, they called their goodbyes to each other. Still exhilarated, they clicked open car doors, minding their sore muscles as they gingerly slid behind steering wheels to head back to the city. Returning to their studio apartments, they took their dogs for quick, efficient walks to nearby Cascade or Denny Park, poop bags in hand. Later, settled on the couch, they scrolled through the day's photos, smiles crossing their faces.

My life, too, had been that way once—not so long ago, a million years ago. The city was Columbus rather than Seattle. My pace, however, was similar. Nick and I, newly married in those years, were absorbed in our graduate studies as much as in each other. Nick started his resident training at the university's large, tertiary care hospital. I worked on my Ph.D. dissertation, sitting at my desk in pajamas in the early mornings while it was still dark outside. Nick lay huddled beneath the blankets, catching a few more minutes of sleep before his next hospital shift beckoned. Shortly after daybreak, we rode our bicycles up tree-lined Neil Avenue from our rented townhouse to the enormous campus of the university. We parted ways at the Medical Center.

"See you later!" Nick called to me over his shoulder and the atmosphere was charged with what the day would bring.

I rode on past the main library to the large, grassy Oval lined with the red brick buildings that housed the liberal arts departments. I sat in art education seminars where my professors discussed art criticism, or the role of technology in the arts, or multicultural aesthetics. Afterwards, with fellow graduate students—Rina and Abdu and Ashley—sipping coffee from McDonalds, we rehashed the material of our seminar. Around us, students sat in clusters beneath great oak trees. Some were engrossed in books while others turned their faces towards the sun to catch the last of the autumn rays.

Two mornings a week I co-taught a course on contemporary art and music with two colleagues from the art education department. The lecture hall was full of boisterous undergraduate students. They sat, wearing Buckeye baseball caps, already restlessly tapping pens on desks. I suspected they had enrolled in the class not so much because of their interest in art and music since the 1950s but because it fulfilled a humanities requirement. Rumors spread across campus that the material covered Elvis Presley and the Beatles, possibly a plus for a required course.

As expected, when "Lucy in the Sky with Diamonds" sounded over the speaker system, the students' bored expressions suddenly shifted, eyes lifted to the recognized melody. Having gained their initial attentiveness, the lectures and discussions moved beyond the Beatles to early rock and bebop jazz, and then to the visual arts, which I knew they would be more hesitant to embrace.

When the abstract expressionists were introduced, skepticism abounded. Balking, they fired their questions. How could a canvas splattered with paint be considered art? What was so difficult about painting a hovering minimalist rectangle? When I showed them Pop Art, they shook their heads at the comic book style of Roy Lichtenstein although they conceded that his technique of using dots was clever. When I projected slides of Andy Warhol's soup cans and Brillo boxes, they simply laughed out loud.

I braced myself for their responses to the next lesson: Earth Art of the

1970s. I flipped photos of Walter de Maria's "Lightning Field" onto the screen. The artist had set up stainless steel poles in a New Mexico field in order to attract lightning bolts, a sculpture best viewed in a storm. The students looked at it, nonplused.

"If I were to organize a field trip to see this artwork, how many of you would come?" I asked hypothetically.

Some of them straightened. A tentative hand went up. The students cast questioning glances at each other. Slowly, one by one, more hands went up. Warmth trickling within me. I was winning them over. Energized, I planned the next lesson.

Most afternoons I worked at the art center, developing instructional materials for art teachers. I drove to Columbus' public schools to deliver glimpses of upcoming contemporary art exhibitions. Enthusiastically, I led groups of all ages through the galleries, thrilled to teach about the artworks I loved. Nothing daunted my momentum. When I returned to our townhouse in the evenings to make a quick spaghetti dinner, I was still rushing from the excitement of my day. I couldn't wait for Nick to come home to tell him of it.

It was a thing of the past. My life, then. Slowly sifting, fading.

On the sidewalk outside, I watched two men in business suits and briefcases stride by my window. A career lifestyle lost to me now. I would have to surrender my life as I had known it. I ran my hand over my thin hair. It was still there, for now. Losing my hair would just be the first of many losses.

My thoughts were disrupted by the return of my friends and my mother.

"We went to Gordon Biersch," Heather recounted, perhaps a little guiltily because I had not been able to join. "And ate Wiener Schnitzel for lunch."

I imagined them sitting at a table for three, talking about the rain in Seattle and Rebecca's travel plans and Heather's upcoming ice carving competitions in the winter. They silently established an allegiance that only persons thrown into a common catastrophe can instantly develop. I saw that some color had returned to my mother's cheeks. I smiled at my friends.

"We brought you something from the store downstairs," my mother said gently. She placed a collection of bandanas and headscarves on the table. I looked at the fabrics, aqua and taupe and green.

"The colors will go well with your eyes," Heather murmured. I grudgingly smiled.

The store on the first floor of the SCCA House was called "Shine." I had peered through its windows on my strolls through the house. Its merchandise was beautifully displayed. Small bamboo plants stood on the windowsills and soft music played in the background. It was a resort boutique at first glance, with its jewelry and greeting cards and books on healthy cooking. Upon closer glance, however, I saw a row of mannequin heads displaying an assortment of wigs—curly, long, blond, dark. Arranged in wicker baskets on the shelves were compression garments, breast prostheses, bras, walking canes. Sensible, functional clothing hung from several stands. Not fashion from Talbots and Ann Taylor and Banana Republic, but comfortable, practical attire comprised of easy-access buttoned shirts, bathrobes, and loose-fitting bottoms. A shopping mall for cancer patients.

I looked at the fabric on the table. In all cultures, over millennia, women wore head coverings. Heads were covered with scarves, veils, bonnets and hats. Reasons for wearing them varied, ranging from church modesty to protection from the weather to fashion. Some followed traditions. Others made statements.

Why was I any different? In the past, I had never spent much time and effort on my hair. A quick brush after showering and I was ready to go. Beauty salons, curling irons and hair dyes had never been priorities. Yet now, my hair mattered immensely.

Rebecca and Heather caught the Sunday evening flight back to Fairbanks. They promised to check in on the children, embracing me tightly just before they departed. After my friends left, the evening fell silent and empty. Another loss.

Across the street, the blue hues of computer screens and television sets reflected in apartment windows. Illness had not factored into those peoples' lives. They lived how I had once, caught up in the pace of my career, never anticipating for even a moment that something like cancer could strike. Would they slow sometimes, spared the hindsight and teachings of a crippling disease, in order to assess the fortune they held by simply being healthy and alive?

Perhaps we weren't in control, as I had always thought myself to be, steering on my personal chosen course. Long ago, I had tacked a quote from an unknown author onto the wall near my desk: "We cannot direct the wind, but we can adjust the sails." I was not so sure anymore.

The next morning, I stood in the bathroom while a friendly, young hairdresser cut off long strands of my hair before shaving my head with a buzzer.

"Your hair color is beautiful," she said.

I looked at my reddish-blond hair pile up on the bathroom tiles. I grimaced in the mirror at my bald head, the pallor of my skin and the sunken shadows of my eyes. I swallowed. Gathering all my reserve, I gave the hairdresser a hug. It could not have been easy for her either.

PART TWO

Permafrost

The temperatures of the Alaskan winter are so cold that, in many areas, there is a deep layer of permanently frozen ground called permafrost that never thaws even in summer.

CHAPTER 15

Raven

"*Kommt gut nach Hause!*" my mother said. *Safe journey home.*

We exchanged quick curbside embraces at Sea-Tac airport, amid the rush of cars, taxis, passengers and bag handlers. Our ways were parting. My mother was returning to Germany with Lufthansa. Nick and I were flying north with Alaska Airlines. Her eyes darted nervously. Disjointed and hurried, she bade us farewell. Her parting wishes, though well meant, were superfluous.

I had been cleared by Dr. Eakins to go home. When the platelets in my blood rose sufficiently and I was somewhat protected from infections, he deemed it safe for me to travel. Nick returned from Alaska to pack my bag and accompany me home. My respite in Alaska would be short, however. I was due back in Seattle in two weeks for my second chemotherapy round. A bone marrow biopsy, scheduled in my oncologist's practice in Fairbanks, would determine the outcome of my first round and evaluate the state of my disease.

I looked after my mother sadly. She turned back towards us and waved from a distance before she was engulfed in the crowd swelling in front of the security check. I had no assurances, no fathoming of my future. My return north did not bring with it a glint of brightness. I was riddled with uncertainty. But I took a deep breath, trying to corral my fear.

Nick and I sat at the very back of the airplane, far away from other passengers harboring possible germs. Nick methodically wiped down my seat, the armrests, tray table, even the window with Clorox wipes. I sat with my eyes closed and tried to think away the ubiquitous pain. It was relentless. Stretching and scouring, it had settled in. Shouldn't the medicines be neutralizing the pain by now? I shifted in my seat but changing position did not help. I breathed through the last swell before the pain gained momentum, intensifying again. I had no sense even of where in my body it resided.

I called forth, behind closed eyelids, the snowscape of Interior Alaska. I wanted to eclipse my harrowing fears. I saw the soothing winter landscape, cool and white. The roads would be packed with snow by now. The winter light of the north falls sideways, slanting through the black spruces. The hills turn crimson in the afternoon, captured in the glow of the setting sun. There is a crunch underfoot, a snap of twigs under duress, a golden cast to the world. For a few moments, I was able to cast aside my discomfort.

We landed in Fairbanks three and a half hours later. The usual shuffle of passengers began, the clatter of overhead bins, the ping of incoming messages on cell phones. I eyed the length of the aisle that stretched endlessly to the front airplane door, where my wheelchair waited.

"Are you undergoing treatment in Seattle?" a flight attendant asked me.

Startled, I looked up at her. She looked meticulous in her navy uniform, handkerchief knotted at her throat, hair pulled back into a bun, lips painted red. She smiled. The headscarf wrapped around my head had given me away. I nodded, miserably.

"Where is your cancer?" the attendant asked quietly.

I thought of blood that carouses everywhere; therefore, my hand motion swept over my entire body. The flight attendant's eyes moistened. She clasped my hand.

"I will pray for you," she said.

I turned my face to the airplane window and the waning light beyond. Am I coming home to die?

Velma Wallis' tale of two old women of the Gwich'in culture of Interior Alaska came to my mind. Sa' and Ch'idzigyaak were abandoned by their people when resources were scarce and the nomadic group needed to move on in order to survive the winter. The old women were left to their own devices. They kept a fire going, caught squirrels and rabbits in traps and made snowshoes from birch and caribou tendons. Sa's advice to Ch'idzigyaak that brutal winter must surely have sounded feeble: "Let us die trying, not sitting."

A shiver went down my spine.

Tara stood at the bottom of the airport elevator, near the baggage carousel. She had come to transport us home. If she was alarmed at the sight of my fragility in the wheelchair, she concealed it well. She gave me a smile, told me she wouldn't hug me for fear of contaminants and said the children were anxiously awaiting me at the house.

"Did you lose all your hair, not just the hair on your head?" Tara asked without preamble as we drove down Airport Way.

"I did," I told her matter-of-factly.

"At least you won't need to shave your legs anymore," she pointed out with a grin. I had to smile at her candor.

At home, Yanni and Helen waited at the doorstep to our house, shifting awkwardly from one leg to the other, not sure how to greet me. Once they digested the sight of their frail mother, they gingerly hugged me. My heart skipped a beat at their sight. Nick's sister Maria stood behind the children. Her face was a conflicting friction of emotions. She looked as though she was either going to laugh hysterically or burst into tears. She made the sign of the cross, muttered something in Greek and shuttled me through the garage up to the living room.

The house looked exactly as we left it four weeks ago. Through the windows I could see the white tundra of the broad Tanana Valley, bathed in silvery late afternoon light. The hills, thickly covered with green spruce, sequentially fell away before us. Ridgepointe Drive and Forrest Road meandered down the hill, covered with snow. In the distance, the Tanana River swept through the valley to its confluence with the Chena River, then on and out of sight beyond the lower ridge near Rosie Creek. Snowmachine tracks crisscrossed the ice on both the Chena and the Tanana River.

Up in the loft overlooking the living room and fireplace, the children and Maria had set up a single bed.

"We thought you might like it here, Mom," Yanni said. "You can see the fireplace."

Helen deposited her favorite stuffed animals next to my pillow. I laid down on the bed fully dressed and closed my eyes, exhausted. I was not hungry, even though Maria had made chicken *avgolemono* soup, one of my favorites, along with a large assortment of other Greek dishes for Nick and the children. I heard the plink of their forks below along with muted conversation.

Pain and fatigue continued their unresolved vendetta. I drifted in and out of sleep. After the children went to bed, Nick sat by my bedside. When his eyes would not hold my gaze, I knew he was not telling me all that was on his mind. My imagination bolted. The air around me suddenly felt depleted. What did he know that he couldn't bring himself to say to me?

Outside the loft window, thick clumps of snow rested on the boughs of the cottonwoods and birches, heavy enough to arch the branches down towards the frozen ground. A weighty snow blanket covered the slope of the hill behind the house. The first snowfall had come early this year.

Towards dusk, the ravens gathered in large roosts for protection and warmth against the falling temperatures. "Croock, croock, croock," punctuated the still air as they tumbled and rolled in the darkening sky.

Watching them, I was repelled and fascinated alike by their antics in the air. Large and black, with razor sharp bills and dark glaring eyes, I could not picture them as the mythic birds they supposedly were. My skin crawled at their sight. Earlier, I saw them rip open the garbage bags that Nick had forgotten in the bed of his pickup truck, ready for transport to the garbage dump. The ravens indiscriminately scavenged and ate the garbage, spilling the contents onto the new powder snow.

Ravens figured prominently in Athabaskan folklore. They were featured, even heralded, in many Alaskan legends. Raven returned the sun and the moon to the people, one account of the story went. A chief stole them for his daughter and hung them in his house, casting the world into darkness. Raven stole the light back by disguising himself and threw the sun and the moon back into the sky. He was able to accomplish good deeds, but he was often cast into the role of a trickster, a keeper of secrets, an antagonist. I tried to imagine what benign spirit could possibly be contained in creatures with such sharp black bills and enormously powerful wings. Their pecking and hopping created pockmarks and rips in the smooth snow blanket. I shuddered. What role would Raven play in my story, one of darkness or light?

CHAPTER 16

Fairbanks at 40° Below

The mercury plummeted to forty degrees below zero overnight. By morning, the frozen world hung in a still, crackling, surreal state. A dense layer of ice fog covered the Tanana Valley. Our house on the ridge hovered right above, suspended, in the clear stillness of the air. The ice fog below looked silvery and soft, but we knew the burning sensation when we drew the biting air into our lungs. We had taught the children to breathe in through their mouths, covered by a scarf or glove. Still, our breath came in sharply the moment we stepped outside.

Determined to be part of normal life again, I pulled on my parka and mittens and shoved my feet into Bearskin boots. "I'm coming too!" I insisted, deliberately ignoring the ache spreading through my back.

"Maybe you should stay home," Nick protested. "It's a deep freeze out there!"

"Pretty typical for this time of year," I retorted and climbed into the passenger seat of his pickup truck. "Come on, or we'll be late!"

The children, bundled up like me, excitedly clambered into the back seat. As we descended down Chena Ridge Road, the ice fog thickened. It was fed by the exhaust of cars in front of us and formed ice crystals in the air. The ice fog was almost blinding in patches. We could barely make out the dim taillights of the car immediately ahead. Sporadically, the ice fog cleared up briefly to reveal the inky dark sky. It would not get light for several hours yet. Yanni and Helen, seemingly oblivious to their surroundings, kept up a steady chatter in the back seat.

"I hope we still have outdoor recess today," Yanni was saying to his sister. Public schools in Fairbanks hardly ever closed for cold temperatures. Only when the thermometer read twenty below were the children summoned inside for recess. I opted not to tell them we were well below that today.

Nick concentrated on the road. "The brakes are stiff," he muttered.

In town, the ice fog was almost impenetrable, even denser than in the hills. Cars, queued up at traffic lights or at drive-through coffee huts, emitted gray clouds of exhaust. Drivers did not want to step out even for a minute to buy a cup of coffee on their way to work. I peered out at the looming buildings that slowly took form just as we came upon them. An eerie yellow glow emanated, caused by artificial light from the windows competing with the thick, grey fog. The world had gone shapeless.

I pulled my parka closer. "The shelters will be full today," I said to Nick.

One could die out there within ten or fifteen minutes without the proper clothing. The Fairbanks Rescue Mission would provide a meal for anyone who needed it, as well as a warm spot to sleep. Winter in Alaska was a wretched time for the homeless.

We were the lucky ones, driving a reliable four-wheel drive vehicle, living in a sturdy home warmed with heating oil. Our children continued their school routine, happily chatting, not even phased by the frigid temperatures. In the parking lot of the Immaculate Conception School, Yanni and Helen climbed out of the car, backpacks strapped on, hats pulled down over their ears. They were soon swallowed in the fog that separated our car from the school's entrance. We could hear them calling to their friends, amorphous, bundled shapes in the gloom.

After Nick drove me home and left for work, the house was too silent to bear. I called softly to Buddy, the golden retriever. I trailed my hand in his silky coat and listened to his pleased grunting. He had been there since the beginning; his arrival coinciding with my diagnosis. Our exuberance of a new puppy's arrival was promptly eclipsed by my horrifying illness. The dog breathed softly into my palm and I let him stay, even though I knew Nick would disapprove of the germs the dog might be harboring.

"We'll go for a walk later," I told him.

His tail thumped when he heard the word, the promise of the outing that in the past was such a typical component of our day. But when I looked at the ice crystals etched into the windowpanes, I felt a wave of fatigue overcome me. I might have to disappoint him after all.

Later, I forced myself up, went to the kitchen to rummage through the pantry for dinner ingredients. I would, at least, try to make a meal for my family. As I opened cans of white navy beans and chopped onions and celery, I felt queasy and shaky again. I perched myself on a bar stool and watched the bean soup simmer while I slowly caught my breath again. Buddy tilted his head, confused at this sudden change in plan.

Nick returned from work earlier than usual that afternoon. "I made the appointment for three," he told me.

He rescheduled his afternoon patients. In the car, he tried to sound matter of fact. "It's something we should have done a long time ago."

Who set up their will when they were in the prime of their life? On an icy day, in the middle of winter? But I said nothing. I thought about the bean soup, knowing that our cozy evening meal with the children was already spoiled.

A secretary showed us into the lawyer's office. "Can I bring you some coffee?" she asked, her eyes straying toward me, then awkwardly away again. I shook my head, my throat too tight to even answer her.

Nick and I sat down in front of a polished desk and waited. The office was tidy and systematically organized. Legal books filled the bookcases. Decorative items hung on the walls; a photograph of Denali reflected in Wonder Lake, a pair of traditional mukluk boots, child sized and beaded and trimmed; a topographical map of Alaska showing the latitude of the Arctic Circle. What remained of the afternoon sun filtered in dimly through the window. I could see the Chena River below. It was only partially frozen because of the heat the power plant not too far downstream gave off. My life had become as precarious as the broken river ice. I needed to cross its groaning, crackling surface. I could, however, at any moment, lose my foothold to plunge below the ice.

The estate lawyer came in, businesslike, folders in hand. He was a tall man with thick glasses. He was wearing, not a suit and tie as I had expected, but a heavy sweater more appropriate for the temperature outside. He placed a large binder on the table separating us and sat down. Without further introductions, he looked directly at me.

"It seems as though we are here to finalize your wills, seeing that your husband will probably outlive you."

A cold fist gripped my heart, wringing it dry.

"No, it's not like that..." Nick was sputtering, coughing.

I heard Nick say something about my chances of survival being high. We were not giving in to statistics.

It took me a few minutes to digest the lawyer's callousness. When I had collected myself to some degree and could breathe again, I signed the necessary paperwork. He was right. My fantasy of living a normal life, as I had known it, had been shattered in an instant.

CHAPTER 17
Aurora Borealis

"Please go!" I commanded.

Nick stood by my bed, next to Andrew, features washed out in resignation. After Andrew gently told me about the dismal outcome of the bone marrow biopsy, confirming that the leukemia was still present even after the harsh regimen of medicines we had thrown in its path, there was little else to say. Even Nick, who just a day ago had told the lawyer that we were not giving in, that we would continue fighting, stood deflated and reduced.

I was consumed suddenly by a great anger, red and hot and glaring.

"Dying of cancer is not an option for me!" I shouted at them, gulping in the suffocating air.

Had everyone given up on me?

Nick and Andrew had discussed my condition without me, weighing options, disheartened. Nick even summoned my friends Rebecca and Tara to come to his practice, where they could meet privately, so they could digest the terrible news together. In town, away from the house, they made plans for me. They arranged for the children, not consulting me, accepting my fate.

Had they all capitulated, unanimously defeated?

I seethed. Surely, there had to be other medicines, different regimens? I needed to return to the hospital in Seattle, undergo more treatment. Why were they proposing finality?

Mutiny and defiance were screaming in my head. Desperate to find someone or something to blame, I fumed. I blamed the messengers, as though they were at fault for my illness. I wanted to thrash and howl, to claw my fingernails into the bed sheets, sobbing and sputtering, but no tears came. I wanted to scream, but my throat seized tight, my voice strangled. I glared at Andrew and Nick as they shuffled out of the room.

After they left, I stared blindly through the window at the stark aspens behind the house. Darkness shrouded the house. I could not leave my young children and my husband behind. How would they cope? Would they scatter my ashes? Would they gather in my name and place a memorial stone that they could visit? Where was I going?

At that moment a shimmer of green stained the night sky outside my window. My tattered breathing quieted a little. I went to stand, in plaid pajamas and bare feet, by the window. The northern lights. They moved forward, across the crest of the hill, undulating in the black sky. Like a wavering curtain they billowed back and forth. The green streak pulsated, like a beating heart, sometimes intense, then paler. The band of light extended all the way down from the ridge into the valley below.

It had been a long time since I saw the aurora borealis. At some point, after having lived in Alaska for years, I stopped looking out for the northern lights every night. When we were new to the Far North, I often listened for the aurora forecast, announced on the radio by the geophysical institute of the University of Alaska.

"Auroral activity will be high tonight. Weather permitting, highly active displays will be visible overhead from Utqiagvik to Fairbanks, possibly as far south as Anchorage."

At night, I breathlessly waited, drawing back curtains, walking from room to room, hoping to catch a glimpse of the light spectacle in the black sky.

"The lights are out" took on an entirely different connotation so far north. The phrase rippled quickly through the community. It was texted on cell phones and pointed out in the night sky. The northern lights were a sparkler, novel and brief. But they had also been in existence for four billion years. An instant. An eternity. Their effect, both ways, was profound.

Fairbanks, because of its location, was perfect for viewing the northern lights. It drew tourists, even in the middle of winter. Once, on a night flight from Seattle to Fairbanks, our airplane teemed with Japanese tourists. They were all intent on attaining the blessing that viewing the northern lights would bestow upon their future offspring. Whether or not this projection was accurate, the moment the pilot announced over the intercom that passengers on the right side of the airplane could view a beautiful display of the northern lights, the Japanese, mostly sitting on the left side, scrambled across the aisle to peer out of the windows. Hand over mouth, they giggled at each other. I thought about hotel rooms in Fairbanks that would surely be booked solid that night.

A combination of the earth's magnetic field, the gases high in the atmosphere, and the interaction of particles streaming from the sun accounted for the physics of the lights. I read about the aurora's location in the ionosphere, fifty miles above the surface of the earth, even though sometimes it looked as though the lights touched the horizon. I learned that the glow of the aurora was due to light emitted from the gases in the earth's high atmosphere when they were struck by electrically charged particles from the sun. The earth's magnetic field guided these particles into the atmosphere near the polar regions, making Alaska a prime spot for viewing the northern lights.

More captivating to me were the meanings ascribed to the lights by different peoples, all trying to make sense of the mysterious phenomenon in the night sky. The legends were as varied as the peoples that construed them. Many accounts were positive. The lights were sometimes seen as ethereal forms of beautiful women who danced with streamers in the sky. In northern Canada, the northern lights were believed to be torches of friendly spirits helping those trying to reach the afterworld. For the Inuit, the lights were celestial manifestations of their dead relatives who were fortunate to live their next life in the sky. According to legend: "Perhaps they are not stars in the sky, but rather openings where our loved ones shine down to let us know they are happy."

Sometimes the lights brought bad news and foreboding. The Eyaks and Tlingits of Southeast Alaska saw the lights as a sign of an approaching battle or a violent death. It was said that the Inupiat considered the aurora dangerous and carried knives to keep it away. A change in the lights' color from green to bright fuchsia could signal someone's death soon after.

Breathe, I told myself, trying to suppress a sudden surge of panic. I peered at the gentle massaging of the color stream in the sky. The meaning of the northern lights would adjust in my favor, I decided. I simply had to believe this.

I made a plan. I could wait for death to overpower me or I could face it up front. Resolutely, I decided that I would not give in. I would take matters into my own hands. Reaching for the phone, I dialed Rebecca's number. When she answered, I demanded to speak to Todd, her husband, not even pausing to explain my reasoning to my friend.

"Did you hear?" I asked Todd, as though the news had already travelled far and wide. "If I return to Seattle, I have a five percent chance of survival."

Todd was silent on the other end.

"I cannot give in to this disease, however slim my chances are." I was almost shouting at him. "Can you to drive me to the airport tomorrow?"

I needed him to respond favorably, as though his neutrality and his absence from the meeting between my husband and my friends could guarantee the implementation of my plan. I waited urgently, breathing hard.

"You bet," came his answer.

CHAPTER 18
7 plus 3

"Fancy going all the way to Alaska in the middle of winter only to return to our balmy climate in Seattle," Steven joked with me.

I had returned to the 7th floor of the University of Washington's Medical Center. In a strangely comforting manner, I was reunited with nurses who had taken care of me during my first round of chemotherapy. They took charge immediately, greeting me as one of their own. I belonged to that floor and there was a certain amount of possession in the nurses' actions.

Ruth had a couple of days off, so settling me back into my room and the hospital routine was left to Steven. He had grown more confident in the last month since he started on the oncology floor. Even though he was still in training, his actions were more assertive, his suggestions more direct. I grew accustomed to his quiet presence. When I needed help in the shower Steven offered his services. I did not give it a thought, as I stood, wobbly and weak, in the shower. I was grateful he was nearby to hand me disinfecting hexachloride wipes and a new change of pajamas. He did not appear to be embarrassed at the sight of my bony body and only laughed when I half drenched him as well with my shower.

Other nurses edged their way into my heart as well.

"Bald is beautiful!" Blayne, on the morning shift, insisted.

I stood at the sink in my room, brushing my teeth, trying to avoid making eye contact with my reflection in the mirror. Blayne noticed and grinned. I spat into the sink, then smiled at her. She had a manner of making me stop feeling sorry for myself.

"Let's go for a walk," Blayne suggested. "I'm heading for the nurse's station. I'll walk with you."

When I returned to my room Kendra, who had been on the night shift, came to reconnect the jumble of tubing on my IV pole.

"I want to tidy it up a bit," she explained to me. "It's not neat."

She looked tired as she worked.

"Long shift last night?" I asked her sympathetically.

"The patient in 724 kept me busy most of the night," she told me with a smile. "But it makes the shift go by faster."

She pulled up a chair, fidgeting with the plastic tubes for much longer than necessary. She told me about her son's soccer game the day before, how she had sliced oranges for the team, about the rain that they had been caught in after half-time. She talked to me well into the morning, long after her shift had come to an end. Did she crave companionship as much as I did? Her empathy was ingrained, a rudiment of her profession.

The nurses were my heroes, the army that had my back, my constant. They instructed me patiently, explaining their ministrations. They fed me and bathed me and walked with me. They sat with me when they sensed I needed someone close by. All of them asked after my children. Not one of them made a remark about my last chemotherapy round that didn't take. In the course of their dealings with blood cancer patients, this appeared to be within the realm of normal. Through them, I slowly began to accept my life's new "normal." I could rely on them to help me bear it.

The medical team, on the other hand, had shifted players during my brief hiatus in Alaska. Dr. Eakins and his team were now treating patients in an outpatient setting, the Seattle Cancer Care Alliance Clinic. In his stead, Dr. Schuster, a stern, practical woman of German descent, was in charge of my second round of chemotherapy.

"You are originally from Germany?" she inquired, while she familiarized herself with my chart.

I tried to sit up in my bed, eager to tell her of my German family. A warm feeling spread through me, much like the one that crept up inside me during summers in Alaska when German tourists frequented and I heard them speak in my native tongue at the grocery store, or at Chena Hot Springs, or in Denali National Park. Nostalgically I followed them through the aisles of Fred Meyer, the supermarket, listening to their exchange. I hoped they would stop me to ask for something, where to find a loaf of bread or how to pay at the self-checkout. Perhaps our conversation would turn to our common nationality. I was always too shy to approach them first.

I wanted to ask Dr. Schuster where her family originated and what had brought her to America but my pain presented itself more acutely then, sharper and deeper. My breath stopped momentarily. My disease was not allowing wistful conversation.

Dr. Schuster eyed me.

"We will use a different regimen this time!" she firmly decided.

Idarubicin would be combined with Cytarabine, which she referred to as Ara-C.

"The treatment is a standard," she explained. "We call it '7 plus 3'. We will give you Idarubicin for the first three days of treatment. At the same time, we will administer Cytarabine, but for a longer period of seven days."

Wearily, I extended my hand for a second time for the consent forms.

Ruth and Steven hooked up the chemotherapy bags soon after Dr. Schuster left the room. Words were left unspoken, yet I sensed that my new life's "normal" was teetering. I watched the nurses busying themselves with the IV, pulling on protective garments, checking my vital signs, starting the drip. I had come to a point of no return. We all knew this round was my last chance.

CHAPTER 19
Denali Fault Earthquake

My laptop, which Nick had left for me on my nightstand, beeped with incoming mail. I miserably stared at the blinking cursor on the computer screen, unable to write back. I did not know what to say.

"You will get through this," Alice, a friend from Ohio, insisted. "This is just a parenthesis in your life. Look at my son. He was diagnosed with a brain tumor when he was young. Now he is living life to the fullest."

I, however, had not arrived at that point yet. I did not possess, as Alice did, the assurance of hindsight. I hit the delete button on the keyboard.

"I don't know why we need to suffer so, except to make us stronger in the end," Richard, another friend, wrote. Who was we? I thought bitterly. It was I that was in this mess, not we. I recoiled from his words, particularly when he inquired whether he and his wife should get tested as possible donors for a bone marrow transplant. With what authority was he proposing that such a transplant was inevitable? I slammed shut the computer.

Irrationally, I prickled at their advice. There was concern in their written lines, in their promises of love and prayers and strength. Still, I stewed. In my present state of mind, I couldn't find the grace to accept them. How could they understand what I was feeling? How could they possibly remain so optimistic in the face of adversity?

My illness was a drama that others could voyeuristically follow at a comfortable distance. Once the sender had dispatched their message, within the detachment of their medium—email, phone message or text—their everyday could return without a backward glance at me. Their consciences appeased, written down within the neutrality of technology, they could turn back to their own affairs. Everyday life could resume.

My life, however, was shaken to the core.

I was reminded of an earthquake that rattled Fairbanks in 2002. It was the year my daughter Helen was born, a child that entered the world in the midst of spring's breakup like a gentle force persuading winter to surrender.

That same year, shortly after midday on a Sunday in early November, the shuddering began. At first the tremble was slight, rousing me from the couch in the living room where I had been resting after I put the baby down for her nap. Within seconds the shaking became more prolonged, more violent. I sat up in alarm. When the wooden Tiki god that decorated the bookshelf behind the couch clattered to the floor along with a crash of books that barely missed my head, I ran upstairs. I snatched Helen from her crib and ran with her in my arms out of the house.

I called out to Tara, who lived across the street, when I saw her emerge from her house as well. We huddled in the middle of the gravel road that separated our houses, reassuring ourselves that the shaking had subsided. Afterwards, we went indoors to inspect the damage.

Books lay scattered. Paintings hung crookedly. Some wine bottles from Nick's cellar under the stairs had broken. Colorful shards spread across the floor. I started sweeping these up with a dustpan and broom when the telephone rang.

"You made the national news!" Jennifer, a friend in Ohio, cried into the telephone. "Are you alright?"

I assured her I was, though I had not turned on the news to hear of the damage.

As I learned later, the earthquake, called the Denali Fault Earthquake, ruptured along its fault in the rugged Alaska Range. An upward thrust cracked open frozen soil and glacial ice. Landslides were triggered in the mountains. Valleys were buried beneath rock and ice. It was so powerful that it set off smaller shocks as far as two thousand miles away. Some accounts stated that the earthquake had been felt even as far south as Seattle and that the water in Lake Union sloshed.

The reportage on the news downplayed the effects the earthquake had on us living in Interior Alaska. The earthquake cracked a 3-foot fissure into the Parks Highway, the main artery connecting Fairbanks and Anchorage.

The news merely reported that it was a good thing there is no major traffic in Alaska. Occurring as it did on a Sunday, most people were home and off the roads anyway.

The Trans-Alaska oil pipeline, which carries thousands of barrels of crude oil from wells at Prudhoe Bay on the North Slope to tankers waiting in Valdez, suffered some minor damage to its supports. Because it was designed to withstand earthquake movement it did not suffer an oil spill. It was closed down for inspection, the news reported, but re-opened soon after. No word was uttered about the economic and environmental disaster an oil spill could have caused.

The earthquake hit a largely unpopulated area of Alaska. People living in the area were generally self-sufficient, maintaining private wells and septic systems. Homes were often heated with wood stoves. No infrastructure was compromised. Very few injuries were reported. The consequences of the earthquake were insignificant.

But to me, standing amid the rubble, the impact of the earthquake was direct and frightening. In many ways, that earthquake was like my cancer. Peoples' response to it was a question of relevance. To the world, in a spectrum of millions of cancer patients, my struggle was just one of many. Mine might just have been another tired cancer story. People looked in upon my plight sympathetically because they could do so from a safe distance, somewhat akin to watching a horror movie from the safety of a movie theater seat.

I thought, absurdly, that everyone would travel the expanse of oceans and land to be by my side. People would come and help in whatever way they could, resolved to tackle this raging disease together with me, no questions asked. I was wrong. Only a handful of people came—my mother, my sister, Nick's sister, and a couple of loyal friends from Alaska.

I tried to condone the others because I understood the expense of travel and the difficulty of missing work. They might have felt awkward in their role as a caretaker. Perhaps I had even discouraged them from coming, understanding their discomfort at addressing the situation at hand. My baldness, my pallor and my malaise had thwarted any invitations. What did one say, after all, to a cancer patient whose prognosis was bleak? On the other hand, deep inside, I knew that I would most certainly have gone to their aid had they been the ones suffering. Where was the gentleness of a hand on my shoulder? Or the reassuring eye contact I craved so desperately? How could an e-mail replace these?

I wanted to scream out loud.

My cancer, too, was a great seismic shift. It was not just some minor event.

The earthquake in Alaska had measured 7.9 on the Richter scale! Tectonic plates had collided. The earth had opened up. My foundation had crumbled. I literally stood with my infant daughter in my arms on the surface of an earth that shook and fissured beneath our feet.

The news, however, reported no damage. All was quiet on the Alaskan front. The world at large had remained unchanged.

CHAPTER 20
Moon Face

"I will only be gone for four days," Nick promised. I could hear the hollowness that had settled in his voice. He stalled as emotion flitted across his face. "I have to go take care of my patients and see to the kids. Tara will be here with you until I return."

I bravely nodded. He needed to fly north, upholding his courage for our children's sake. Fortitude trailing and concentration dithering, he would sit in examining rooms with his patients, listening to their grievances when all he felt was the weight of his own despair. Bringing home a pizza from the Great Alaska Pizza Company or Chinese food from Pagodas, he absentmindedly listened to the children across the dinner table while they ate. His thoughts were in Seattle because he could never be sure of what he would encounter on his return.

Before leaving, Nick held my eyes in a steady gaze. "I love you," he fiercely whispered.

His endearment drowned me in a flood of unease. The words, in our seventeen years of marriage, had never sounded so urgent before.

A passage by the poet Kahlil Gibran came to my mind. "One day you will ask me, which is more important, my life or yours? I will say mine. And you will walk away not knowing that you are my life."

He is an extension of myself, like a limb taken for granted when running a marathon or a song understood in utter silence. Even in his absence, he would be with me. I would tell Nick this when he returned.

Catching me in my pining, Tara arrived.

"We've decided that we will not leave you alone for even one minute," she announced, bustling into the hospital room. "Between all of us, there will always be a caretaker with you."

I smiled at her but knew that the burden of my illness was shouldered by only a few. I was glad to see my friend. At the same time, a terrible sadness engulfed me.

Tara busied herself around my hospital room. She shoved the reclining armchair into the corner by the window where she intended to sit and watch over me. She stashed her briefcase and computer into the cupboard alongside my change of pajamas. She was moving in. I watched her arrange cards on my nightstand that our children had drawn. She pinned up a collage of photos, mostly summer scenes in Alaska, and tacked them to the bulletin board at the foot of my bed. The assembled photos spelled out the word LOVE. Beneath her usual stoic façade, I caught a glimpse of fragility.

"Do you remember Antarctica?" Tara reminisced, smiling and pointing at a photo in the collage. Our children, ranging in age from three to eleven, were dressed in shorts and rubber breakup boots. They posed in a group near Nome Creek in the White Mountains. It was our first camping trip of the spring on Memorial Day weekend at Mount Prindle campground. The air was still crisp and remnant snow patches dotted the mountain slopes. On one of these the children stood. They had, ironically, named it "Antarctica."

There was a photo of Nick and Tara's husband Wes grilling on our deck overlooking the Tanana Valley, with wine glasses in hand and spirits uplifted to begin a long evening under the midnight sun. Another picture portrayed Yanni, Helen and me, dressed in red T-shirts and numbered bibs, after the "Beat Beethoven" 5-kilometer run. That year we had managed to complete the course before the playing of Beethoven's fifth symphony, bellowing out from loudspeakers and car radios parked along the roads on the University of Alaska's campus, came to an end. With huge grins the three of us looked into the camera, clutching symphony tickets in our hands, the reward for our achievement. There was a photo of Nick napping on the couch in our living room with our dog Buddy at his feet.

Tears stung behind my eyes.

Just then Dr. Schuster walked into the room with her medical students. Noticing the collage on the bulletin board, they delayed addressing my medical issues and asked about Alaska instead. Does it really get 50 below in the winter? Is it true there is no night in the summer? How far is Fairbanks from the Arctic Circle? And which is it, the grizzly or the black bear, that cannot climb a tree?

"No, not everyone lives in igloos," Tara smiled, bolstered by their interest. "Our houses are on the slopes of the Chena Ridge and they are built of wood. But we do have triple paned windows because of the cold."

She grinned when Dr. Schuster inquired about Sarah Palin, former governor of Alaska, who had run as the Republican vice-presidential candidate alongside Senator John McCain two years before. "Yup. She still lives in Wasilla."

Tara described encounters with moose that often amble along the streets of Fairbanks. She told them about Chena Hot Springs to which we fled in the winter when the temperatures dropped so we could sit in the sulfuric rock pool and break off the tips of our frozen hair. She told them about camping in the White Mountains and picking blueberries near Cleary Summit in the fall. I listened, too tired to partake in the conversation. My pain had not lessened but, for once, I was not heeding it attention. It was comforting to hear Tara describe the place we called home.

Eventually, Dr. Schuster steered the conversation back to my health.

"Your cells looked sticky underneath the microscope. We will perform a lumbar puncture. I want to make sure that no abnormal cells have spread to the brain or spinal cord."

A searing pain ripped through me again, as though in response to her announcement. I winced and drew in my breath.

"I will return later this afternoon," Dr. Schuster decided. "We can do the spinal tap right here in your room."

Just before leaving the room, she turned back and looked at me critically. "How bad is the pain?"

I grimaced, trying to think of the right adjective. Intense. Frayed. Glaring.

Dr. Schuster pointed to a pain management chart that hung on the back of the door. On it, yellow emoji faces ranged the scale. Bright smile, distressed frown, cross-eyed howl.

"Can you indicate your level of pain?" Dr. Schuster asked me.

I pointed at a face clenching its teeth near the top of the chart.

Moments later, on Dr. Schuster's order, Ruth wheeled a patient-controlled analgesia pump into my room.

"You need to stay on top of the pain!" Ruth said sternly. She set up the pump next to my bed. My pain had reached a point where even potent pain medications like Oxycodone and Oxycontin did little to lessen its acuteness. Jagged bolts alternated with spreading gnawing throughout my body. I held my breath when the stabbing jolts came. I exhaled through the darting pain.

The PCA pump allowed me to infuse pain medication into my port at the click of a button.

"It's not possible to accidentally give yourself too much medicine," Ruth explained. "The pump is programmed to allot only two pumps every ten minutes. But you must use it *before* the pain becomes intolerable."

She needn't have worried. I double clicked the pump button the moment I was allowed to, wishing I could continue clicking forever to make the pain subside. Then I fervently counted the minutes to ten.

Dr. Schuster returned in the afternoon to perform the lumbar puncture. Steven, who was measuring my temperature, asked whether he could be present. He had never witnessed a lumbar puncture before. I turned sideways on my bed and drew my knees to my chest in order to widen the spaces between my vertebrae so that she could collect the cerebrospinal fluid. I concentrated on Steven's face as he sat beside me, holding my hand. His eyes followed Dr. Schuster's maneuvering behind me. I remembered Nick telling me about his own first lumbar puncture at the Ohio State University Medical Center. He was a second-year medical student, ready to insert the needle while the attending physician stood beside him giving him quiet prompts. Later, Nick told me that he felt strong resistance and was surprised at the force he had needed to exert to insert the needle into the spinal column. I saw Steven twitch slightly and knew Dr. Schuster had arrived at exactly that point in the procedure.

"Try to lie flat for an hour. That way you won't develop a headache," Dr. Schuster advised before she left the room.

My second round of chemotherapy brought on symptoms of early menopause. After a torrential and unexpected bleeding that was to be my last menstrual period, I experienced no more menstrual cycles. Instead, I drenched pajama after pajama because of scorching hot flashes that subsided only occasionally. Several times during the night I rang the bell affixed to my bed for Kendra, the night nurse, to bring me new clothing, new sheets and a washcloth to wipe the perspiration off my body.

Caught between hot flashes and radiating pain in my bones, I snapped at Tara irritably. Tara gave no sign of being vexed. She busied herself with learning the routine of the hospital. Within a day, she knew all of the nurses assigned to my care by name and soon became part of the 7th floor family. She found the linen cupboard in the hallway and brought me towels, Chapstick and non-skid socks. When she figured out that the only appealing taste to my non-existent taste buds was, strangely enough, orange soda, she hiked through the neighborhood surrounding the hospital in search of any beverage that tasted like Fanta. When I drifted off to sleep, she worked on her computer, revising proposals and meeting deadlines. When I was awake, she read to me anecdotes of Yanni's and Helen's activities from the online Cozy Calendar that Rebecca in Fairbanks had set up to keep us all connected. Not once did Tara let on that being by my side kept her from important tasks or her own family.

Still, she must have secretly sighed when Nick returned from Alaska and walked into my hospital room. Dr. Schuster and her students, grouped together at the end of my bed, were sifting through my chart. The students were regurgitating my condition, my medications, summarizing the events of the past few days.

Nick took one long look at me. "Birgit has developed a blood clot."

All eyes were immediately fixed on me. Preoccupied with my chart, huddled in a circle, no one else had noticed. I had, indeed, developed a "moon face." My head was tremendously swollen. A flurry of activity ensued. Dr. Schuster inspected my neck and determined the clot was on the right side. The medical students wheeled an ambulatory ultrasound machine into my room to confirm this.

"Deep vein thrombosis and pulmonary emboli are particularly

dangerous in patients with leukemia," Dr. Schuster informed them. "What is the preferred method of treatment?"

"Blood thinners?" one of the students suggested.

"Warfarin can be taken in pill form but can take several days to reach a therapeutic level," the other student proposed. "How about Heparin? We could infuse it through her port. It has the advantage of being able to immediately thin the blood."

I followed their discussion, feeling like a patient in a "House" episode on TV, a rat in a medical experiment. In the end, it was decided that I would be placed on a Heparin drip, given the severity of my situation, and then I would transition to giving myself Lovenox anticoagulation injections into whatever abdominal fat I had left on my stomach. I looked to Nick, still standing at the foot of my bed. He looked like he had aged twenty years since he left. I finally greeted him with a stunted smile.

CHAPTER 21

Thanksgiving Ice Storm

I kept my eyes fixed on the pedestrian crossing on the street below. I could see Pacific Street, the main thoroughfare in front of the hospital entrance and the University of Washington campus. A bike path ran alongside the road, lined with large oak trees that had turned crimson. Runners in sleek tights and headphones sped by, their pace frenetic enough to make me long for it and sigh simultaneously. Nick and the children would walk down the same bike path from the Silver Cloud Inn any moment now.

Because of my blood clot, Dr. Schuster decided that I should remain an inpatient for the Thanksgiving holiday. Instead of returning to Alaska for the holiday, I would remain in Seattle.

"But we've already made plans for Thanksgiving dinner," I argued feebly "Our friends are going to help us put it all together. We already booked the flights."

Dr. Schuster, determined, was not giving in. "Your condition is too serious. We will do the next bone marrow biopsy here, in your room, in a couple of days."

No kitchen redolent with smells of turkey and stuffing, no decorated table with autumn colored place mats and wine glasses, no hugs at the front door. My favorite holiday, with my children, was dashed to pieces.

Nick, seeing my fallen countenance, quickly suggested: "Let's fly the kids here. We'll make our own Thanksgiving."

The flight was quickly organized. It was a change of plans, but one we still had control over. I brightened.

I suddenly caught sight of them on the sidewalk below. My family stood at the pedestrian crossing, waiting for the green light to change to red. Helen appeared taller to me, dressed in a pink and white ski jacket that she saw at Beaver Sports in Fairbanks and had wanted for some time. She was gesturing, asking her father something, eager to cross. Yanni stood quietly, taking in the enormity of the hospital in front of him.

What felt like a gust of wind swept through the room, creating an ensuing silence. For a moment, a sense of being past everything cloaked me, a feeling that was primary and rooted deep. My gaze was locked on the three people below. I felt something steady within me, holding its place. For a few moments, I was calm. And then, just as quickly as it enveloped me, the feeling was gone again. The hospital noises in the hallway were audible again. My stomach ached. My throat was raw with bile.

"Can I spend the night here with Mom?" Yanni asked, moments later, when they all stood around my bed, gowned and masked in yellow protective clothing.

"No, I want to," his sister chimed in at once. "Can I, Dad?"

Turns would be taken, they decided. Never before had they all so desperately wanted to stay with me. Unease rose and circulated within me.

"We'll let Yanni stay first, since he's older," Nick decided.

Seeing Helen's crestfallen face, he quickly added, "And you and I will go to Blue C Sushi for dinner."

The corners of Helen's mouth turned up. She shared a taste for gourmet food with her father. Nick's eyes met mine above her head as something unspoken passed between us.

"And tomorrow morning we'll all reconvene here," he said firmly just before they took their leave.

"Friends" was on TV that night. Yanni cackled at the dialogue in between mouthfuls of his ham and cheese sandwich, which was brought up from the hospital cafeteria along with chicken soup for me. When Blayne, the nurse on night shift, came in to check my vital signs, Yanni told her at length about the hockey team he was playing on.

"We are called the Arctic Lions. We played the Anchorage teams and we beat all but one. I think we will play in the State Cup."

Blayne was satisfyingly impressed. She helped him unfold the sleeping cot and gave him a pillow and blanket. She pointed out that if he needed the bathroom there was one down the hall by the nurse's station. Yanni fell asleep as soon as his head touched the pillow. I, however, lay beside him, listening to his lengthened breathing, and looked at his features that had softened in sleep. I remembered the baby he had been. Not so long ago you were a dream in my own sleep, I whispered to him.

We were aroused abruptly the next morning by Helen. She came running into the room, yellow mask dangling in her hand.

"We're going to the Boeing factory!" she exploded, grinning. "Dad's taking us!"

She was working on a science fair project about the 787 Dreamliner for school. Her research consisted of a tour of the factory in nearby Everett where the airplanes' final assembly took place.

"The airplanes are made of a new material," she explained earnestly. "It's called composite. It makes them lighter and they don't need as much fuel to fly."

She described angled wingtips, a smooth nose and wider seats, all distinguishing features of the airplane. Listening, I felt a surge of pride.

Thanksgiving dinner was turkey sandwiches from the hospital cafeteria. My family ate beside my bed. I watched, unable to stomach anything myself. Yanni and Helen chattered. Nick's face held the reflection of a smile as he listened. Our peace was temporary. For now, however, it was enough.

One Thanksgiving in Alaska, several years ago, an ice storm captured us. It left Interior Alaska paralyzed. The National Weather Service meteorologists, following the storm's track inland from the Bering Sea, warned of its severity and cautioned Interior Alaskans to prepare for it. It was not the snow that was the primary concern. Fairbanksans were typically braced for snow accumulation. It was the forecast of 40-mile-per-hour winds in an area that is known for its calm conditions that was worrisome. Trees, already burdened and bent under snow loads, could topple in such gusts. Ice on power lines could result in long lasting power outages.

As predicted, that year's ice storm crippled even the most stoic Alaskans. All the roads turned to ice, impassable and dangerous. Schools and offices were closed. The hospital treated only the most necessary cases. No one came or went on account of the ice. Yanni and Helen nicknamed our driveway "the luge" and slid, hooting and hollering, down the slippery incline on their sleds. The ice creaked. The branches of the spruces glittered.

Nick, in the kitchen, rummaged through the refrigerator and pantry to devise a Thanksgiving dinner that we could put together with what we had at hand. Our planned gathering of friends, with everyone bringing a part of the meal, was called off. Upstairs, I ran the water faucet to fill up the bathtub. We would have no electricity for a stretch of days. The jet pump would be unable to pump water through the pipes. The house would quickly lose heat. I rounded up flashlights, candles and extra blankets. I carried logs from the woodshed behind the house and filled the bins on the fireplace hearth. I placed a shovel, emergency blanket, tow strap and jumper cables into Nick's four-wheel drive pickup truck, in case we needed to leave the house. With all preparations made, we huddled together by the fire and waited.

Suddenly, we heard a noise at the top of our driveway that resounded in the otherwise eerie silence of the neighborhood.

"Hellooooo the house!" came a holler down the driveway.

Our friends Elizabeth and Brett arrived with chains on their car tires and ice cleats on their boots. They lugged between them a bag containing the Thanksgiving turkey they had roasted, determined to celebrate the holiday with us, ice storm or not. They were not giving in to the landscape claimed by the icy deep freeze. We were Alaskans, after all, prepared to deal with hindrances in our course. We would simply make it work. We ate turkey by the fireplace that evening, laughing and talking well into the night, even after the lights went out.

CHAPTER 22
Remission

On Sunday evening, well after rounds were completed and I thought only the night shift was on the hospital floor, Dr. Schuster walked into my hospital room.

Her usually stern features dissolved into a wide smile.

"You are in remission!" she announced. "The result of your last bone marrow biopsy shows no evidence of disease."

Nick and I stared hard at her.

"Smile," she laughed, when she saw our blank expressions. "This is good news."

I looked at my husband, too afraid to rejoice.

"There are no leukemic cells detectable in your blood stream at present," Dr. Schuster explained.

I allowed myself a diluted smile. I reached for Nick's hand.

"However," Dr. Schuster quickly added. "Remission does not mean cure. It simply means that no abnormal cells can be detected by medical tests such as a bone marrow biopsy."

I was confused.

She called it remission; an uncertain state, when symptoms retreat for a period, but lurk just beneath the surface. The disease could return at any time.

"You will have to continue another three cycles of chemotherapy, called consolidation rounds," Dr. Schuster emphasized. "These are aimed at killing any remaining leukemic cells that might still be present at a microscopic level."

I was not done yet.

Dr. Schuster pulled out a chart logging the times I pressed the button of the PCA pump. Vaguely, I remembered when I started to feel the pain lessen. I had given little thought to its coinciding with the number of times I pressed the button on the pump. The pain had slowly tapered off in the last few days. The intervals between clicks had lengthened.

"It shows us the exact time frame of you going into remission," Dr. Schuster explained brightly. Victoriously, she pointed at a mark on the graph. "This is when you stopped using the pain pump altogether. That's when we got the upper hand over the disease."

Nick looked at me, but his smile was preoccupied. Immediately, my fear billowed again. I registered the uncertainty of being in a state of remission. It had been a close call. Dr. Schuster's elated reaction testified to that. My hold on life was still so fragile.

CHAPTER 23
Winter Solstice Fire

The enormous gym went quiet. Twenty pairs of eyes rested on me, taking in my sunken cheekbones, my hollow eyes, my sweatpants and the headscarf tied around my bald head. I had driven to the Immaculate Conception School. I planned to slip in, quickly write a check, and return to the car in the parking lot, ignition still running, unnoticed by any students. When I walked towards the gym, I rounded the corner and walked straight into Yanni's sixth grade class. Holding basketballs, in knee length gym shorts and sneakers, they were lined up for their physical education class.

I cringed, stomach squeezed tight. They all knew. They had heard the rumors. Now, I stood there, in confirmation. I was ill. I had been in Seattle for treatment. The unimaginable cancer had afflicted, onto a classmate's mother nevertheless, one of their own. I had imagined, somehow, that things would be different on my return. People wouldn't regard me differently. I would return to Fairbanks for my respite, carry on like usual, driving the children to school, paying the tuition bill. But everything had changed. I was a curiosity, a person sidestepping normal life, someone to be admired and pitied at the same time. I was no longer Yanni's and Helen's mom, simply dropping them at school, like so many other parents did on a daily basis. I was now an anomaly, a kink in the usual flow of life.

Yanni's voice came towards me from the end of the queue. "Hi Mom!"

I held my breath, afraid of causing him embarrassment. Twenty pairs of eyes were now diverted to him instead of me, registering his matter of factness, his acceptance of me. Their awkwardness shifted and settled. Voices, once again, filled the space. And I fled from the gym, drenched with love for my son.

That afternoon, in return for his rescue, I agreed to drive to North

Pole to watch Yanni's hockey game even though the chill of the rink was displeasing to me even in the best of conditions. The small Alaskan town of North Pole, a community east of Fairbanks, was an attraction for tourists. It conveyed quaintness and the spirit of Christmas in streets that were named Mistletoe Road and St. Nicholas Drive and Snowman Lane. Lampposts, in the form of red and white striped candy canes, lined the roundabouts. Behind the Santa Claus House, crammed with ornaments and gifts year-round, reindeer nuzzled at visitors through the fence of their pen.

Our destination was Polar Ice, the ice rink, a lesser aesthetic. The rectangular building, clad in dull brown siding, resembled an oversized garage. Inside, the temperature was kept markedly low, not only to preserve the ice in optimal condition but also to maintain the disgruntled state of the spectators. I pulled on my coat and gloves before even entering the building. Climbing the stairs to the balcony overlooking the ice, I joined other parents watching from above. I felt their looks, cast obliquely. I kept my own gaze steadfastly in front of me. I had returned. Unlike the outright stares of Yanni's classmates in the gym, the parents at the rink masked their curiosity, stealing glances before turning their attention back to the hockey game. The clatter of sticks, the waft of sweaty gear from the player bench below, the cheers and groans from the spectator bench brought with it a sense of my former life. I felt strangely abstracted from it. As though I had not yet earned the right to be part of it again.

When my legs wobbled, I sat down on the metal spectator bench. My red blood cells had not yet reached their normal levels. I sat, catching my breath, weakened by the effort it had cost me to climb the stairs. A friend approached. Sam noticed me from the string of spectators on the balcony. He came to sit on the cold metal bench next to me.

"It's good to see you here again," he smiled. "You made a lot of people very happy."

He had an amiable approach. Just a few years beyond me in age, a million ahead in experience, I listened to his words. I knew he was talking about my remission, my presence at the hockey game, my attempt to be part of everyday life again. His words carried weight. He, too, had experienced cancer in his immediate family.

"Does it get better?" I asked him.

He looked at me and there was a trace of sadness in his eyes. He squeezed my hand before we both turned our eyes to the hockey game.

Cancer held me captive in a time frame that did not constitute normal life. I hovered at the edges, looking in upon the course of the unfolding days, but felt as though I had no business being part of them. The house, the children, the grocery store, the dog, returning to work: all beckoned for me to resume. Nothing, however, was like before.

After the hockey game, at home again, I spent a long time looking out over the snowy landscape. Snow sifted from the Siberian larches and drifted, effortlessly, down the incline of the hill behind the house.

The people of Alaska had a multitude of ways to describe snow: air thick with snow, newly drifting snow, hard crusty snow, first snowfall, spread out snow, glazed snow in a thaw, snow on clothes, rippled surface of snow, very soft snow, sugar snow, salt-like snow, snow that can be broken through, snowdrift that blocks, snow blown in under a doorstep, snow used for a specific purpose. Snow could tell stories. More so than merely inform about pressure systems and precipitation levels, it beckoned for us to respond to it, to heed its advice, to pay it particular attention. It could change its appearance, its consistency and its texture from one moment to the next. It appeared altered to us at different times of day: metallic in the early morning, golden in the evening. Often, it soothed and stilled. It could be a cleanser, gently blanketing the world, covering impurities, like a great equalizer.

Other times, it could be deceptive and vague. On the hill behind our house the snow lay thick and even, undisturbed, seemingly serene. Beneath thick layers of snow, rare winter wildfires sometimes ignite in Alaska. These "holdover fires" were leftovers from the summer and could survive the long Alaskan winter beneath the snow layer. Smoldering, they could eventually come back to life. They were kept alive by dead plant material in the soil or squirrel middens. These could provide just enough fuel to keep the fire alive. On occasion, given a burst of oxygen, the fire could explode back into life.

Would my disease be like a rare winter wildfire: hibernating, latent, rekindling? Or could I count on the perfectly planed snow cover to snuff out any smoldering remains of my cancer?

CHAPTER 24
Corridor Walk

"Why do you choose to work on the oncology floor?" I asked Ruth.

She was concentrating on flushing heparin through the port in my chest, but her answer came without hesitation.

"There is something special and different about cancer patients," she told me, her eyes flickering up to mine. "Their hope is often feeble, but they are always grateful for what they have."

I had returned to the hospital in Seattle in order to start my first consolidation chemotherapy. The goal was to solidify my state of remission, to make certain the disease was driven out of the last nooks and crannies of my body. When I arrived, I was admitted to the 8th floor rather than the 7th. I looked about myself, confused. A nurse I didn't know came into the room with my admission paperwork.

"Aren't you a 'new leuk'?" she asked, surprised at my composure.

I sat on the bed, legs dangling from its side, flipping through a People Magazine. She braced herself for the anguished questions of a patient newly diagnosed with leukemia. I shook my head.

"First consolidation round. I'm in remission."

The nurse breathed audibly.

The absence of omnipotent pain in my body was novel. I had almost forgotten how it felt. I could flex my calf muscles without cringing and roll over onto my side without groaning. I slept for a full night without back pain ripping me out of my sleep. My mood lifted. I even smiled at the nurse when she handed me the consent forms.

"Dr. Eakins is assigned to your care again," she informed me, looking at the clipboard in her hands. "He is ordering the same '7 plus 3' regimen again. Why mess with success, right?"

I wondered whether Dr. Eakins had taken issue with the fact that it was Dr. Schuster's medicines, rather than his own proposed trial combination of drugs, that put me into remission. I handed the consent forms back to the nurse when Ruth, my former nurse, bustled into my room.

"You are part of the 7th floor," she announced in greeting, grinning. "I'm having you transferred downstairs again."

There was a mix-up in the paperwork. Ruth saw to my relocation. Warmth spread within me. Our bond went beyond hospital administration and room delegations.

When I was settled back into a room on the 7th floor, I told Ruth about the evening in Fairbanks when Nick and Andrew sat at my bedside and outlined my dismal prognosis.

"I wasn't giving in," I said, feeling the sudden prick of tears behind my eyes. "I had to give it a fight. I needed to give it a chance, don't you think?"

Ruth nodded, pragmatically. "That is why you are in remission now," she said, quietly. Her certainty was solid.

My resolve the next morning was to build myself up again. I tried not to think about the debilitating effects the chemotherapy drugs would have on me in the next few days. I wanted to concentrate instead on being in remission and read about my disease, something I had not had the energy or courage to do until now. I would inform myself about statistics and relapse rates. I heard the doctors and medical students discuss my condition daily but did not want to research my cancer online. I refused to google WebMD to type in the name of my leukemia or bookmark relevant websites. I walked quickly past the journal rack in the hallway, filled with pamphlets that outlined cancers, ones I could not bring myself to read. I avoided online blogs about other cancer patients' experiences. I shunned Internet sites that offered support groups. Now, I felt ready to absorb the information, to listen to the conversations the doctors carried on. I would take control.

I reached for the laptop. Different types of leukemia afflicted patients. My particular type was called acute myeloid, or acute myelogenous, or acute myelocytic. Often it was abbreviated to AML. I did not have the medical knowledge to interpret the adjectives. But I understood the common denominator: acute. The disease would progress quickly. It was always fatal if not successfully treated. I shuddered and quickly read on.

There were other types of leukemia. Chronic myelogenous leukemia, or CML, also afflicted predominantly adults. CML could lie smoldering for several months or even years before the cells grew rapidly enough for symptoms to develop. Treatment options included what doctors called "watchful waiting." The patient was closely monitored, but treatment was postponed. Was this leukemia the better one to have? What would it be like, I wondered, to live with the fear that, at any moment, the leukemia could grow erratically into the accelerated state of AML before it could even be controlled again? Patients with CML did have one advantage over patients with AML like myself. A drug had been developed, in the form of a daily pill, to suppress the disease. Even though it would never completely eradicate the fear of the leukemia escalating, patients with CML at least had some control over the disease. No such drug existed for me.

I toggled through the screen and read on. The 5-year survival rate for patients with AML was 27 percent. I went cold inside. Only 27 percent of people diagnosed with my disease were still alive after five years. Only one in four patients survived. I had barely made it through two months. My finger trembled as I moved the cursor down the screen. How would I make it to five years? I did not want to read more but could not bring myself to stop.

There existed leukemias that occur in children. Acute lymphocytic leukemia, or ALL, was a common type found in children although they could also develop the acute myelogenous type. I thought of young children feeling the pain I had experienced, of being prodded with needles, of being confined to a hospital bed, of coping with the odds. Disheartened, I closed my computer.

I went for a corridor walk instead. Pushing my IV pole in slippers and a hospital robe, I noticed other patients' circumstances. I rounded the first corner and came upon a family—father, his grown children, grandparents—all huddled outside a newly arrived patient's room. They held each other, desolate, their tears raw. They must have just heard the news of the patient's diagnosis and were reeling from its implications. When I approached, they gathered themselves momentarily, sniffing, wiping at their cheeks and turning away. Their discomfort at my sight was evident. I shuffled by, offered them a sympathetic glance, even a small smile. I was, after all, already two chemotherapy rounds ahead of them.

I picked up my pace. The IV pole rattled over the tiles. A young, tall woman walked the length of the hallway ahead of me with long, confident strides. Her mother, just as long legged, walked alongside, but needed to offer her daughter no assistance. In fact, only the headscarf on the younger woman's head gave away the fact that she was the patient. Her skin glowed a healthy color. Her blue eyes were fixed on some point a few paces before her, shuttering out the world. Her mouth was set in a firm line, her attention focused on some inner source.

"Who are they?" I asked Blayne when I reached the nurse's station. Their strength towered far beyond their physical height.

Blayne winked at me. "Can't talk about them," she said. "You know, HIPAA privacy laws."

I turned away, disappointed. I wanted to know at what stage of treatment the young woman was. Perhaps it was a plausible goal for me as well.

"You know," Blayne called after me as I moved on, "Inner strength goes a long way towards healing."

I noticed a room at the end of the hallway. Double doors insulated a vestibule containing a hand washing station, protective gowns and masks. The vestibule led to the patient's room. Someone in an extremely delicate, immunocompromised state, I thought. I could not get even a glimpse of the patient through the double doors. A note affixed to the outer door asked visitors to stop by the nurse's station before entering. The sedatives the patient was receiving, the note said, were allowing the patient some rest.

The patient's wife sat on a metal folding chair in the hallway. Her slate grey expression carried the look of a worn-out caregiver. She smiled at me when I rumbled by with my IV pole.

"How are you feeling today?" she asked gingerly.

It was a rhetorical question that I had come to despise, but her friendliness was not lost on me. "Fine," I answered, ridiculously.

I parked my IV pole by her chair. Her name was Jane. She had travelled with her sick husband from New Zealand to receive treatment at the University of Washington Medical Center.

"He researched numerous cancer centers and hospitals prior to his bone marrow transplant," Jane said with a vanquished expression. She pulled out a handkerchief and dabbed at her eyes. "He will remain behind the double doors for a whole month,"

Her husband had relapsed from his state of remission three times.

CHAPTER 25

Sundogs and Diamond Dust

"We need to have a Christmas tree!" Helen exclaimed, looking around the small apartment shortly after she and Yanni arrived.

Nick and I made eye contact with each other. Plants and flowers were not even permitted in the Seattle Cancer Care Alliance House. The smell of Clorox cleaner hung in the air. Bare windows, sterile walls, and bright lights cast the room into sharp contours. No wreath, fragrant with pine needles, adorned the door. No colorful stockings hung from the fireplace mantelpiece. No waft of baking came from the oven.

I had moved back into the SCCA House after being discharged from the hospital, to a small apartment on the third floor this time. On Pontius Avenue below, storefronts and apartment windows were decorated with twinkling lights. People walked the sidewalk, bundled up and laden with colorful gift bags. They paused at the coffee shop across the street for a latte or a macchiato. Under normal circumstances, my apartment's location would have been ideal for Christmas shopping. Even if I felt strong enough, I was still too immunocompromised from my last chemotherapy to walk into department stores, filled with circulating bacteria and sneezing people. Instead, I sat by my window, sifted through catalogs and purchased my children's Christmas gifts online. I had them delivered and hid them in the back of my closet.

Helen dropped her bag near the bed and sat down sullenly. No cheery embrace for me. Her brother, standing behind her, eyed the situation warily as he looked around the small apartment. Christmas, this year, would be nothing like it typically was. On their way up to the apartment, they noticed a large, beautifully decorated Christmas tree set up in the communal living room of the house. An Indian family had already "borrowed" it and was in the process of piling brightly wrapped presents beneath it. Cancer, evidently, obfuscates cultural boundaries and religious traditions. Weren't Indians predominantly Hindus and Muslims? Helen stared at the Indian family and pouted.

It was Nick who managed to rescue the situation. The tables in the second-floor dining room were bedecked with fake miniature trees made of green plastic and draped with silvery tinsel. Seeing Helen's face, Nick promptly walked into the dining room and confiscated a miniature tree for our apartment. Triumphantly, he set it onto our dining table. Helen, cheered again, ran to get white copy paper, scissors and scotch tape from the reception office downstairs. She sat down immediately at the dining table to cut out stars and taped her decorations to the otherwise unadorned windows. I watched her from my armchair, grateful for the adaptability of her youth.

In years past, in Alaska, we had always tried to incorporate my German heritage into Christmas. It was a special holiday, one whose traditions I took great measures to maintain. A package, sent by my mother from Germany every year, launched my nostalgia. I unpacked marzipan and *Lebkuchen*, gingerbread made with honey, fruit peel and spices. I arranged small tree candles onto the boughs of our fir tree, to the fascination and unease of our American friends who already envisioned the house going up in flames. A wooden, hand-carved nativity scene complete with shepherds and magi and the *Christkind* which my father had bought for us one year in the Bavarian town of Oberammergau, was set on the fireplace hearth. An Advent wreath, crafted from pine branches and cones and decorated with four pillar candles, counted down the Sundays before Christmas. On the evening before Christmas, we often gathered with our friends around the dinner table, listened to Händel's *Messiah* and Bach's *Weihnachtsoratorium* and waited for the roasted duck to emerge from the oven. For dessert we ate *Stollenkuchen* and drank *Glühwein*, a mulled wine fragrant with spices, rum and sugar.

A lump formed in my throat. I longed for home as much as Helen did. At this time of year in Alaska, the first sundogs of the season appeared like Christmas lights of the Far North. Low on the horizon, they appeared as shimmering orbs in the sky, an optical phenomenon of the frozen north.

On extremely cold days, ice crystals formed close to the earth's surface. The crystals in the atmosphere, sometimes referred to as diamond dust, could fall and bend in the sunlight, causing a refracted image of the sun to appear on either side of the sun. The part of the sundog closest to the sun often shimmered red. The outer edges sometimes appeared greenish-blue.

"It looks like there are three suns," Helen remarked the last time we saw them.

I had parked the car on the side of Friar's Way, at a pullout overlooking the valley, so we could gaze at the shimmering orbs. Below us, the morning fog was rising off the Tanana River. The hills behind us were just barely rimmed in pale pink. The sundogs, balancing the fuzzy sun, hovered. It took no longer than fifteen minutes before they sifted away again.

"They are called parahelia," I told Helen, engrossed in the ice show. "The Greek word means 'beside the sun'. They look like haloes, don't you think?"

She absorbed this as she crunched on a granola bar.

I noticed sundogs many times before but never stopped to think about them. The winter was speaking to us. Sundogs were generally thought to be good indicators that weather conditions were likely to change. In which direction, however, remained part of their mystical ways. Perhaps it was not just the weather changing but change on a more profound level. What was it the sundogs prophesied? Was a circle around the sun a bad omen, as some believed? Or a sign of positive change? Helen and I gazed at the symbols in the sky until they dissolved into the haze surrounding them.

Christmas Eve came without ceremony. Dinner consisted of hamburgers Nick brought back to the apartment from a nearby 13 Coins restaurant, along with soup for me. It was a modest celebration, but I was awash with sentiment. We all slept together that night, on an assortment of cots, pull out sofas and beds. I listened to Yanni and Helen as they settled into sleep and was comforted by Nick's presence as he sat reading by a small lamp. I was in remission. My third round had been "unremarkable." Even though we all grasped that what is taken for granted is not the same as what is granted, for tonight it sufficed that we could drift into sleep together.

I awoke later than I intended the next morning. I meant to stealthily prop the children's wrapped gifts next to the miniature Christmas tree on the table. Helen, up early, already discovered them in the back of the closet. She blinked at me with wet eyes.

It was the year Helen learned the truth about Santa Claus. He faded as quickly as the sun haloes in Alaska had into diamond dust.

CHAPTER 26
The Cowbell

I emerged from the elevator into the lobby to the sound of a loud, clanking bell. My friend Laura, tall and smiling, jangled it vigorously. She looked exactly like I remembered her: broad smile, with sandy hair falling in waves around her face. Her family stood next to her, grinning. The children, Maverick and Sarah, had grown so tall that my heart skipped a beat. Greg, her husband, remained unchanged.

"Does this bring back memories?" Laura laughed, ringing the bell again.

I embraced my old friends.

Laura and Greg used the same cowbell in Alaska some years ago. When Rebecca and I ran our first half Marathon, along a combination of paved roads, dirt trails and bicycle paths in the town of North Pole, Greg and Laura cheered us on. Laura drove her minivan to different spots on the racecourse. Whenever they caught sight of us, they scrambled out, hollering their encouragement and jangled the cowbell wildly. Rebecca and I, half delirious after many miles of running, smiled each time we saw them.

Laura and Greg and their children lived across the street from us in Fairbanks, in a single-storied blue house that was tucked back into the woods. Our children grew up together, learning how to ride bicycles on the dirt road that was Locksley Court, climbing around in Sarah's playroom castle, stringing up a badminton net on their lawn. Once, they dug a hole in the front lawn to create an ornamental pond with the intention of keeping fish, but which was ultimately quite out of character in the surrounding, straggly wilderness. In the long summer days, Laura prepared elaborate picnics to take along as she combed the neighborhood blueberry patches with plastic containers and a group of spirited children. In the winter, when darkness encroached early in the afternoon, she gathered them into her house to scrapbook or to bake cookies or paint the walls of the playroom Teletubby blue.

The afternoon in the communal living room of the SCCA House passed quickly. Remnant raindrops trailed down the windowpanes. Periodically, the sun tried breaking free from the cloud cover. The cityscape revealed itself from the mistiness, hesitantly, only to be doused again by the next rain shower. We tried to catch up on the two years since they left Alaska in the hour and a half I had before my next infusion appointment. I inquired about their move to Illinois, asking question after question, stalling. I wanted the conversation to remain light, steeped in comfortable memories. I knew that eventually they would circle back to my illness, my predicament. I would not be able to guard them from distress.

"We love Carbondale," Greg told me, describing the town they now lived in. "But we still miss Alaska."

Laura had taken on a new position as a hospice nurse. Maverick's favorite pastime was assembling parts of old cars into an operational vehicle. Sarah told me at length about her cat. I sighed and tried to remember why we had not kept in touch more consistently.

When our time together drew to an end, Greg asked "What's in store for you? Now that you are in remission, will you be able to go home after your consolidation treatment and be done?"

I shrugged. I turned to look out of the window, averting eye contact. Outside, the rain was now prickling off the sidewalks with some force. They all looked at me inquiringly.

"The doctors are telling me to think about a bone marrow transplant," I finally conceded, raggedly. "I have been pushing away the idea."

I could not soften the news, either for them or myself.

"What would that entail?" Laura asked carefully.

Maverick and Sarah had gone still. They shifted, uncomfortably, on the couch.

"It's risky," I told them. "Not all patients survive the transplant. If they do, the side effects are sometimes so awful that they wish they hadn't."

I waited to let this information settle. Silent and fretful, they waited for me to go on.

"It is a little like taking my chance up front," I explained. "I have a 50/50 chance of surviving the transplant. Or, I could 'watch and wait' and pray for no relapse."

The family digested this. I looked at them miserably, hoping for some words in return, a reassurance, a softer place to fall. The room was so quiet I could hear the beat of my own pulse. I looked at the clock and got up. It was time for my next appointment, my chance to escape. The family got to their feet awkwardly.

"Thank you," Greg said quietly as he hugged me in parting. "We know this visit was more for us than for you."

I looked at them earnestly then.

"Transplant or not," I told them, trying to put some steel into my voice. "My type of cancer is treatable and curable. I'm going for the cure!"

Laura wiped away a tear that had escaped onto her cheek. She jangled the cowbell again.

Deep down, even if I had not grasped it rationally yet, I knew that I would, indeed, start another marathon, this time one not of my own choosing. And they were still rooting for me.

CHAPTER 27
Yukon Quest

"Let's go watch the start of the Yukon Quest," I suggested.

The children looked at me skeptically. My illness showed itself in spurts during my recovery at home. Some days seemed almost normal. When my energy level held steady, activities were planned. Yanni and Helen hesitated.

"Come on," I laughed. "Get your coats and mittens!"

In the few days allotted to me before my next consolidation round in Seattle, I occupied myself with the passage of winter rituals in Fairbanks. The length of the winter set Alaskans apart from the rest of the world. The year, so far north, spanned eight months of whiteness. Alaskans embraced a multitude of winter activities: snowmachining, ice skating, skijoring, cross country and downhill skiing, ice fishing, hockey, ice sculpting, snowshoeing. Rather than being a time of endurance or lengthy darkness, winter's possibilities were unending. The brevity of the day had to be made use of. That was winter's only condition.

I, too, wanted to push my distressing thoughts of a possible bone marrow transplant out of my mind, to free myself at least for a few days. I wanted to engage in the winter activities of the north like I always had.

February marked the start of the dog mushing season. On the frozen Chena River in downtown Fairbanks, a sizable crowd of spectators had gathered at the starting chute of the Yukon Quest dogsled race. Mushers with frosted eyelashes and fur-trimmed hoods queued up with their dogs and sleds. Their dog handlers held back the barking dogs with effort. In teams of six or ten or fourteen, the dogs jumped and yanked against their harnesses, eager to be on their way. Their panting breath formed clouds in the air.

Yanni and Helen squirmed in anticipation. Suddenly, the first dog team was off. We cheered along with the other spectators. The dogs scampered and ran, pulling mushers and sleds beneath the bridges spanning the frozen Chena River to the outskirts of town and into the wilderness beyond. The mushers, sliding past us at regular intervals, wore heavy parkas, thick mittens and numbered bibs. They stood on the footboards of their sleds, raising a hand in parting, an acknowledgment of support, a gesture of pride.

"Huskies are great runners," Yanni observed. The dogs, surprisingly small, were all muscle and stamina. "The dog handler over there told me the dogs are the real athletes in the race."

I felt Helen's gloved hand pull at my coat sleeve.

"Where will they sleep tonight?" she asked. "Will the booties and dog jackets keep them warm?"

I followed her gaze as the dog teams, one by one, pulled out of the chute. Darkness was already blanketing the outlines of the buildings on the riverbank. Lights glowed behind curtained windows. The dog teams continued running through the frigid blackness. The hiss of the sled's runners, the crunch of snow and the dogs' panting were the only sounds in an otherwise vast silence. For six or eight hours they ran, until they got to some type of shelter to rest: a checkpoint, a cabin, a camp. The musher heated food for the dogs in steaming bowls, took off booties to rub ointment onto paws and rubbed down sore muscles before bedding them onto straw for a few hours before their next run. It was only after the dogs had been attended to that the musher found his or her own rest.

Some provisions would have already been made for the racers. Bush planes delivered dozens of bags of food for both mushers and dogs to various checkpoints along the trail—Circle, Eagle, Dawson City, Pelly Crossing. At checkpoints, helpers and veterinarians were at hand for assistance and emergencies. For the most part, however, musher and dogs were on their own, left to their own devices. Alone in the roadless north, they travelled on rivers, lakes, marshes and bogs that were frozen solid. The trail retraced the historic backcountry travel route of the 1890s Klondike Gold Rush era between Fairbanks, Dawson City and Whitehorse which miners, trappers and mail carriers used. Like them, mushers and dogs had to rely on themselves on their thousand-mile trek through the harsh Alaskan and Canadian wilderness.

It was a difficult journey. The trail crossed frozen rivers, streams packed with jumbled ice and frozen, bumpy tussocks on the tundra. It skirted isolated northern villages and climbed mountains with names such as King Solomon's Dome and Eagle Summit and Rosebud Summit. Temperatures could drop sharply. Winds penetrated fiercely at the higher elevations.

I recalled the writer Hudson Stuck, at the turn of the century, who wrote about dog mushing in *Ten Thousand Miles with a Dog Sled*. His experience of being out alone in the wilderness, exposed and vulnerable, had changed little over the years. Life was all about time, or the lack thereof.

When we sat at our cozy kitchen table with hot cups of cocoa later on, I listened to the children talk about dog booties and mushers and sleds in high-pitched voices. A shadow fell over me. This was what life before cancer had been like. An excursion, a memory, cheeks still reddened from the cold, the bark of the dogs still in their ears. It had only taken a few moments. Its imprint, however, would last a lifetime.

My time, just like the musher and his dogs in the wilderness, was also measured. Musher and dogs raced against time, but also with it, as they practiced an art of a time gone by, when sled dogs and mushing were integral to village life in Alaska, whether for travel or trapping or hunting. Replaced nowadays by snowmachines, mushing had diminished, almost disappeared, in rural villages. In the great race of the north, however, its essence was preserved, its spirit very much alive.

For me, too, time was calculated. It was of little importance when it moved sluggishly during my hospitalizations. But time was also my most treasured commodity when day after day slipped past: I was a chronologist of the number of times that I would be able to return north to be again in the surroundings that captivated me, together with the people I loved. Time was friend and foe alike, divided into a time before cancer, and the present. The length of the winter did not trouble me because in the back of my mind was the unsettling notion that there might be no more winters to cherish beyond this one.

Perhaps I had to think earnestly about the bone marrow transplant. I owed it to my children. Maybe I needed to take the risk, to give it my best shot, so that we could all resume our lives without cancer lurking at every moment. Maybe we could even move beyond the constant timekeeping and watchfulness, to a time beyond cancer's limits and ends.

    I thought of the tenacity and strength of the musher and dogs as they faced the difficult terrain they intended to conquer. Theirs was a different quest, but I was also built of that fabric. I, too, would not scratch from the race. In the grip of winter that year, I felt something akin to hope.

CHAPTER 28

Neutropenic Fever

My headache developed in the evening. I tried hard to disregard it. The day, thus far, had been very pleasant. By nightfall, however, I could no longer ignore the painful pulses in my head.

Tara and I had taken a short walk earlier that day in the neighborhood surrounding the SCCA House. The streets were lined with red brick, tightly adjoining residential apartments, fronted by pebbled flower boxes and small veranda staircases. Beyond Minor Avenue, a view of the downtown high rises opened up. Angled and tiered in succession, their glass fronted facades glinted in the morning sun.

Cascade Park lay quietly in the morning light. The wood chipped playground was devoid at that early hour of children's laughter. The large, grassy area still awaited park frequenters to play softball or throw a Frisbee for a dog. A homeless man, bundled in a hoody and grimy blanket, had curled up beneath a large oak tree, wrapped in the desolation of a disadvantaged life. Beyond him, the park was deserted.

In the community garden patch next to the park, Tara and I looked at the shriveled, brown foliage of the vegetables and flowers that plot owners would coax into an outburst of color and fruit in the coming spring.

"Rosemary, hollyhock, azalea, iris, Pacific crabapple," Tara pointed out.

Even though it was late February, the mildness of the winter in Seattle allowed us to identify the leaves. Tara, who was an avid gardener and able to produce a flowering garden even in Alaska, told me about the vegetation indigenous to western Washington. It felt good to be outdoors. We sat on a park bench in our coats and breathed in the scent of wet mulch and pine trees.

My last chemotherapy round had passed without incident. I returned to Seattle with my newly acquired confidence, ready to tackle my final chemotherapy round. My cells were still free of leukemia. Perhaps I was not "resistant to treatment" after all. I felt buoyant, as I hadn't in a long time. I almost wanted to thumb my nose at the doctors and the hospital as I inhaled the possibility of life after cancer. Perhaps because of my stronger disposition and at Tara's insistence, Nick agreed to return to Alaska early, to attend to the needs of his patients and our children while I stayed behind with Tara to recuperate.

Magnanimously, I smiled at him. "Go home and be with the kids. I'll be alright here."

Tara worked on her computer after our walk while I strolled around the house. In the vacant exercise room, I looked at the two stationary bicycles. Eager to move my muscles again, I climbed onto one of them. Wearing pajama bottoms, a sweatshirt and slippers, I nevertheless managed to pedal for twenty minutes.

Outside, rain clouds scudded. It started to drizzle. When Tara and I walked to the clinic for my scheduled red blood cell infusion in the afternoon, rain cascaded in a fine mist from our umbrellas. I insisted on walking the distance, determined to regain my strength, even though cresting the hill on Mercer Street left me panting.

My infusion lasted longer than usual. Tara and I watched reruns of "Little House on the Prairie" while we waited for the trickle to end. It was dark by the time we walked back. On Eastlake Avenue, the headlights of a constant stream of evening rush hour cars glared. Neither the rain nor the rushing traffic dampened my mood. I was content, glad to be out of the clinic. The weekend lay ahead. I had no scheduled appointments. Tara and I bantered as we walked, commenting on passersby like old college friends going out to the campus pub on a Friday night.

Bolstered because I felt a little better, I suggested we stop at Mad Pizza on Thomas Street for dinner. Even though my immune system was still compromised, Tara reluctantly agreed. She ordered a Mediterranean pizza pie and I, on a whim, asked for a glass of red wine. Out in public on such a rare occasion, I settled myself contently to people watch and listen to the conversations around me. A group of women, dressed in slim fitting Lulu Lemon pants, trendy tops and scarves, perched themselves on barstools surrounding a high table. All four sat texting on their cell phones, oblivious to each other. A husband and wife, seated at a table nearby, exchanged practicalities. Did he pick up the dry cleaning? Had she managed to stop by the bank today?

Tara and I joked as we hurried home in the rain after dinner.

"Did you hear the woman back there? Complaining about every minor inconvenience of life? The rain, her work schedule, her kids."

"You can't really do anything about it," Tara decided. "So you may as well just get on with it and worry about the things you can actually change."

"People don't realize how good life is," I answered philosophically. "Until something like cancer hits. It's enough to pull your hair out!"

Tara looked at me and smirked. "But you don't have any hair to pull out!"

Torn between laughter and dismay, I laughed so hard that my stomach muscles ached and tears welled up in my eyes. I had to shake my head to reassure Tara that all was well.

However, not long after we returned to my apartment, my temples started to throb. The rain pelting at the window resounded loudly in my head, a cacophony of drumming.

"I'm going to lay down," I told Tara.

Still smiling from our joke, she nodded and settled herself on the couch with her computer. I climbed into bed and drew the bedcovers over me. Chills started. Perhaps I had overdone it today: the walk through the community garden, pedaling on the stationary bike in the exercise room, walking the distance to the clinic.

"Do we have any Tylenol?" I asked Tara.

She glanced up immediately, smile erased. A moment later she stood by my bed, thermometer in hand. When she looked at the results, Tara promptly picked up her cell phone to call Nick in Alaska.

"Birgit's developed a fever," her voice was tinged with anxiety, "101.4."

I looked up sharply, heartbeat quickening. It was actually happening.

The very thing the doctors had wanted to ward off at all costs. A neutropenic fever. An infection was setting in when my body had virtually no white cells to counteract an attack.

Nick's voice sounded shrill, clearly audible across the room. I could hear him give Tara urgent instructions. The decibel level of his voice revealed his concern.

"Give it half an hour. Then measure her temperature again. And call me."

The second reading showed a temperature of 102°. Slowly rising. This time, he told her to hang up and call a cab at once. "No," he said. "An ambulance!"

Tara dialed 911 immediately. Hurriedly, she started stuffing clothing into a bag, darting glances at me. Medications, pajamas, toothbrush, underwear. I sat on the side of my bed, jittery and weakened. My hands trembled as I tried to tie the shoelaces of my sneakers. It took an enormous effort.

We took the elevator down to the lobby to wait for the ambulance. The lobby was empty, save for a receptionist working late in an office behind the counter. His desk lamp glowed eerily in the otherwise dark lobby. He did not seem surprised when the ambulance arrived, lights flashing. Emergencies, evidently, were routine at the SCCA House.

Moments later, two paramedics in dark blue cargo pants and sweatshirts rolled a gurney into the lobby. One of them sat down next to me on the couch, clipboard in hand, and started asking me questions. When did the headache start? What medications was I taking? How far along was I in my treatment? I answered, befuddled, because my head was pulsating, crushing against its confines.

Tara stood next to me, on the phone again with Nick, nodding. "Yes, I'll do that," she said to him, again and again.

The ambulance sped through the dark, rainy streets of Seattle, the red and blue glow reflecting off the glistening asphalt. I looked at Tara's waxen, grave face beside me and understood the responsibility she, all of a sudden, had on her hands because of me.

"They are not even sounding the sirens," I tried to flimsily joke. "What a cheat!"

Tara gave me a droopy smile.

I broke out into a cold sweat. My friend could not help me now. I was being rushed to the emergency room. This was serious.

The emergency department at the University of Washington Medical Center was a tumult of white lab coats, gurneys, curtained cubicles and beeping monitors. Was there a full moon? I asked myself, sensing the flurry and agitation around me. Nick had once told me about a superstition that circulates among hospitals and medical practices. It equated maladies and emergencies with the completion of the lunar cycle. Hospital admissions spiked. Births climaxed. Traumas escalated.

A medical orderly parked my gurney in the hallway alongside another patient also strapped to hers. Tara stood next to me, taking in the activity around us. I found myself suspended in a grey zone, suddenly very tired, wanting to shut out the hammering in my head. The woman on the gurney next to me was coughing fitfully. I saw anxiety creep over Tara's features.

"Excuse me!" she called after a nurse that hurried by.

"We need some help!" she repeated to another.

Everyone was otherwise preoccupied. Her cell phone rang. Nick, on the other end, demanded an update and insisted she find a doctor immediately. There was not a minute to lose. The patient next to me continued her hacking.

Suddenly losing her calm, Tara grabbed the next person in green scrubs that passed us. She yanked his nametag closer to her.

"Darren!" she exploded. "That woman over there is coughing up a lung! My friend cannot be here! She's neutropenic!"

Her outburst caused Darren to look at me. He took in my demeanor while Tara shoved her cell phone into his hand and told him to talk to Nick. The conversation was brief. The doctor listened to Nick's frantic explanations, then waved over a passing orderly.

"Direct admit!" he decided without hesitation.

CHAPTER 29
The Choice

The shapeless room came back into focus two days later. Contours slowly took form. Nick and Tara, jumping up from their bedside chairs, looked at me anxiously. A nurse came into the room at once to check my vital signs when he saw that I was awake.

I looked from my husband to my friend to the nurse, bewildered.

"How long was I sleeping?" I asked them, trying to concentrate.

"Through my entire shift," the nurse told me, pumping up my blood pressure cuff. "Yesterday and today! Don't do that to me again, please!"

Nick's apprehensive expression segued into one of relief.

"An infection set in," he explained, reaching for my hand. "The doctors have been treating you with antibiotics, but those have little effect when you are neutropenic."

"When did you come?" I uttered, confused. "Where are the kids?"

Nick booked himself onto the next flight out of Fairbanks, depositing the children with Rebecca. Barely reining in his panic, he tore to the airport in the middle of the night, cursing the fact that Alaska was so far away from the Lower 48 States. It would take hours before he was with me. In his haste, he left the front door unlocked, all lights in the house on and the dishwasher running.

At the same time, in Seattle, Tara sat by my bed, vexed and fretting, awaiting his arrival. Throughout the night, they told me I spiked temperatures as high as 104.7. I thrashed feverishly on the bed, incoherently muttering, in some delirium of my own making.

My blood cultures came back positive for strep viridans bacteremia, an infection that often inflicts the blood of neutropenic patients. In the early morning hours, the doctor on call decided that the Infectious Diseases department needed to be consulted. I had begun what was called a "non-productive" cough. He ordered a chest x-ray and a CT scan, concerned about possible pneumonia. Medicines were added to the regimen I was already on: Ceftazidime, Acyclovir, Fluconazole, Ciprofloxacin, Vancomycin.

Hearing all this, I looked at Nick and Tara, stunned. I was placed on five new medications. Blood cultures were taken. I even had an x-ray and a CT scan performed on me. In my febrile state, I flailed through all of it, completely unaware. It was as though I had plunged into a river in Alaska, heavy with glacial sediment, a current so thick it was pulling me under. And then, while the swirling water still threatened to engulf me, blood rushing in my ears, I grasped something—a branch, a rock, a gravel bar—something solid I could claw my fingers around. I surfaced, gasping and sputtering.

Nick was talking to my family in Germany on the phone.

"She's awake," I heard him say as he peered at me from where he stood by the window. Face turned, voice muted, he mumbled. "For now, she's doing alright. I'll call you with updates." He then went in search of the doctor on call.

Tara pulled up a chair next to my bed. I thought of my parents and siblings, much too far away at that moment. I imagined their terrified thoughts, their feeble pacing by the telephone, their helplessness in matters at hand. I had sent everyone into a panic. I wanted to show Tara that I was better, in control again. I got out of bed to use the bathroom. Even the three or four paces to the bathroom door were an exertion. I was reaching for the railing next to the toilet when my pajama bottoms slid off my hips. I gazed down at them, pooled at my feet. I tried to reclaim some semblance of dignity.

"I just lost my pants!" I turned back to Tara, trying to joke.

Tara lost no moment to brightly reply, "At least you are wearing underwear! I wouldn't be!"

I gave her an impoverished smile. Who was it, I thought, that wrote a real friend is one who walks in when the rest of the world walks out? I couldn't remember.

We sat for a long time that afternoon, absorbed in our own thoughts, deflated after our scare. Swiftly, life had turned around on me. I tasted defeat clearly for the first time. My clutch on health was tenuous. With a sinking feeling, I realized that I would move about my days gingerly from now on, always alert, readying myself for another downfall, another relapse. My "non-existent disease" would forever have a strong hold over me. I needed to make my choice. Perhaps the bone marrow transplant was the only option left to overcome this precarious state of existence I found myself in.

Tara rebooked her flight for later that night. While she waited to board the airplane to Fairbanks at SeaTac airport she sat at the bar at Anthony's, eating halibut tacos and watching the evening news. Whitney Houston died that day, drowned in her bathtub, Tara told me over the phone. Drugs, most likely, everyone at the bar was saying.

Hot tears welled in my eyes as I grappled with the irony. I was trying so hard to simply stay alive while others, sprawling and boozing, were gambling with the privilege of a healthy body. My options were growing slim. The choice of a bone marrow transplant was becoming no choice at all.

PART THREE

Arctic Breakup

Springtime in Alaska, a time of year when the frozen rivers break apart and flow again.

CHAPTER 30
Arctic Breakup

Alaska was in breakup. The silvery winter light slowly gave way to an amber glow in the mornings. Much later than the rest of the world, straggly brown patches of earth appeared beneath the snow blanket. In the dry climate of Interior Alaska, the snow dissipated slowly into the atmosphere rather than slush down the roads and hillsides. Muddy dirt roads, emerging after many months of winter, softened in the meager sunshine during the day, then refroze into hardened ruts at night. The earth smelled of softness, mud and trodden lichen. Yanni and Helen wore breakup boots on their way to school, squishing their feet first into the black mud, then streaking them through remnant snow patches. Nick's pickup truck was covered in grime.

Nick and I drove down the Parks Highway with no real destination in mind, only an urge to be outside. We absorbed the landscape in its thaw. In years past we often drove down a rutted logging road to the river's very edge so we could listen to great boulders of jumbled ice crash loudly and vehemently against each other in their breaking. The river was still frozen but shifting already, splintering and rupturing beneath the surface. It wouldn't be long before the ice went out.

"The tripod will trip any day now," I observed when we reached the bridge that crossed the Tanana River near the small Alaskan town of Nenana. We looked down upon the river ice. The black and white tripod, set up in the middle of the river, looked miniscule in the huge landscape. Over the years, a lottery had been designed by winter weary Alaskans. In anticipation of the long-awaited spring, residents across the state bought lottery tickets and recorded on them the exact time they thought the ice would break in the Tanana River. Utilizing their knowledge of ice thickness, the duration of cold snaps and sheer luck, the guess that came closest to the time of the actual break up won. Everyone watched as the ice shifted for the first time, triggering a clock that recorded the precise moment the tripod toppled. With much fanfare, some lucky winners were announced every year.

We were playing a lottery game of our own this year. We had turned the argument over in our heads. Like the fits and starts of the unpredictable spring temperatures, our thoughts were cast first in one direction, then in the other.

"It is a matter of taking our chances up front," Nick reasoned the night before, as we stood in the kitchen washing our dinner dishes. "The transplant is dangerous, but if we make it through, we're done."

The light was faltering outside, though it was only early evening. A fire crackled in the fireplace in the living room, warding off the spring chill that still accompanied the nights.

"But we have already thought this through," I argued, clattering the plates into the drying rack. "The chemotherapy has done its job. Am I not in a solid remission?"

I looked at Nick, irritated. There was a quiver in his cheek. He put down the dishtowel he was holding.

"You did not go into remission in your first round," he said quietly. "We need to consider that." He had put on his doctor voice.

"But that was because of the trial meds Dr. Eakins put me on," I counteracted. I turned off the water faucet and turned to face him directly. "If he had started me on the '7 plus 3' drugs like Dr. Schuster did in my second round I would have gone into remission right away."

Nick looked towards the fire in the living room. He placed both hands on the kitchen counter and took a deep breath.

"We also need to remember that you have received close to your lifetime dose of Idarubicin," he continued, not looking at me. "That was probably the medication that was most useful in terms of getting the leukemia under control. Taking it again risks cardiac toxicity. Should you relapse, we won't have any great tools to suppress the disease again."

It was a solid argument, but still one I did not want to abide by. I continued to argue.

"Any discussion of transplant would be superfluous had I gone into remission in my first round," I persisted, though a little more feebly now.

I followed his gaze to the flames, licking and quivering, against the stones of the hearth. And the neutropenic fever? It was a setback, but I had bounced back from that as well, hadn't I? I wilted even more.

Nick sighed, rubbing his temple.

I went upstairs to bed soon after, illogically angry with Nick, hollow at myself. Before dawn, early Sunday morning, while the children and Nick were still asleep and the time gap between America and Germany offered the opportunity, I crept down the staircase again and dialed my parents' number.

"I'm done," I told them brightly. "The chemotherapy is behind me."

"*Das hoffen wir alle*," my mother spoke loudly for the benefit of my hard hearing father next to her. *We all hope for this.* A crackle sounded, static in the telephone line. She paused. "*Deine Entscheidung ist bestimmt die Richtige.*" *Your decision is surely the right one.*

Did I hear doubt in her voice? Nettled, I hung up. Why could she not reassure me in the manner she had always done throughout my childhood? Why was everyone so skeptical, so unsure that I was well again?

When we drove back to Fairbanks from Nenana, we did so in silence, caught up in our own thoughts. We were still vexed from our conversation the night before. The drive had done little to soothe, to stabilize.

"I'm taking Buddy for a walk," I announced to Nick when he pulled the car into the garage. I grabbed the dog leash, pulled on boots and called to the dog. The sun had warmed up the day amid the sounds of icicles dripping from branches and of snow slabs sliding off the roof. I breathed in the air that smelled of snow and mud patches. Rivulets of water channeled down the driveway. Buddy and I took the loop road down Ridgepointe, then onto a four-wheeler trail that led steeply uphill through undeveloped land. On the edge of the woods, I could see the expanse of the valley spread before me: the peaks of Mount Deborah and Hess and Hayes, the rivers, the boreal forest.

My confidence, meager the night before, was bolstered again. The banks of the Chena and Tanana rivers had reemerged from the crusted snowbank. Along the hillsides, the birch trees shimmered green. Soft pussy willows clung to stark branches. On Creamer's field, Canada geese and sandhill cranes with an uncanny sense of direction and timing during their migration, landed between the ploughed snowdrifts. Spring was slowly returning to Alaska. I watched Buddy run ahead, sniffing at earth patches, bounding vigorously up the hillside along the trail, his nose twitching with the smell of wet spruce.

Again, I went over the argument in my head, going over the rationale against a bone marrow transplant logically, in painstaking detail. Explaining my reasoning to myself cemented the certainty of my decision. Without others to contradict me, I told myself that a bone marrow transplant was not needed. I would continue as I was, going for walks, watching the seasons progress. I was captured in the promise of lengthened days, the faith in a season restoring life to the frozen North.

I saw Andrew, my oncologist, a few days later. He came into the examining room, stethoscope dangling around his neck, his smile warm. I felt comfortable. We had known each other for a long time, a camaraderie first established through Nick and Andrew's professional acquaintance. We spent my allotted appointment time discussing our children who were transitioning into junior high school soon, spelling out the advantages of sending them to West Valley High School rather than remaining at the Catholic School. Andrew asked whether I would be returning to the University of Alaska in the autumn, where I had taught in the art history and German language departments. We chatted amiably about Skiland, the slopes on Cleary Summit which afforded broad views of the White Mountains and about how long the ski season would still last this year.

A knock came on the examining room door. A nurse's head appeared around the door. "Could you take a phone call from another physician?" she asked.

"I'll be back momentarily," Andrew said, uncrossing his legs to get up, apologizing for the interruption.

I waited beneath the brightly lit fluorescent lights. The prints on the exam room's walls were by Claire Fejes, an Alaskan artist whose subject matter often depicted scenes of the Athabaskan culture. In one scene, the abstracted, geometric forms showed a woman and little girl with baskets of blueberries. Their complexions, in brown and ochre tones, were like the earthy landscape behind them. The woman's and child's curved backs, bent over to pick blueberries in the tundra, were echoed in the shape of the hills. A blue and lavender sky hung above. The scene was tranquil.

That was when I noticed my medical chart, still open to Andrew's last notes, on the table next to the blood pressure cuff. For a split second, in an instant that would shape my destiny, I hesitated and asked myself whether I should read his note. Then I peered closer.

"High risk for recurrence AML."

The words on the chart note hit me like a punch in the stomach. The room whirled and spun around me. I grabbed onto the armrest of my chair to steady myself. An iciness crept over my entire body. I had been deceiving myself. I shook my head, slowly, from side to side, and closed my eyes. What had I been telling myself? I would not stay in remission. The risk of my disease returning was high and probable. There it stood, boldfaced, in black pen, permanently recorded.

Something inside me broke and crumbled. I yanked my coat from the hanger and let myself out of the examining room. Panting, I hurried by the medical assistant at the front desk, who looked up in surprise.

"I'll call to reschedule," I muttered. All I could think of was to get to the safety of my home.

I cried silently as I drove home, tears running uselessly down my cheeks. Greyness had crept into the day. Behind the gilded spring day, every uncertainty loomed. Beguiling, as it had warmed up, the afternoon threatened snow showers again. All my glimpses of hope were relentlessly shattered.

CHAPTER 31
Fifty/Fifty

"You may call me Iolanda," the Rumanian doctor smiled as she shook our hands. "It's my first name, but a little easier to pronounce than my surname."

She motioned towards the polished conference table at the center of the room. Its surface gleamed in the sunshine coming in through the window. In a flowerbed just outside, yellow daffodils and blue hyacinths were swaying gently in the breeze. Iolanda spoke with an accent, even though she had lived in America for many years and was an instrumental physician of the Seattle Cancer Care Alliance. She had curly blond hair, narrow set eyes and the tendency to spit a little when she spoke.

Nick and I had returned to Seattle for a bone marrow transplant consultation, sitting close together at the table across from her, in a weighty silence. The words in Andrew's chart still hung in the air in front of me, brutally stark and unambiguous. My delusion was stripped. Denial was not possible anymore. I would not be celebrating the end of my chemotherapy. I did not need to question anyone anymore, as I had in the last few weeks—doctors, nurses, friends, counselors, nutritionists—riddled with uncertainty. I knew what my next step had to be.

Laying on the conference table was my massive medical chart, divided into an "A" and "B" binder because of its extensive contents. Another three-ring binder contained the consent packet for a bone marrow transplant.

"We have two options," Iolanda chose her words carefully, causing her to pause in between sentences. She spoke with surgical precision. "One is to stop treatment now that Birgit has finished her consolidation rounds and watch long-term for any indication of recurrence. The other is to undergo a bone marrow transplant, which has its own risks, but has the ultimate potential of curing the disease."

Nick and I sat silently, hands clasped.

"I will explain the process of a bone marrow transplant to you," she continued. "First, a suitable donor needs to be found. This task is neither straightforward nor easy."

She looked directly at me. "We have already completed the human leukocyte antigen typing of your three siblings in Germany. Unfortunately, none of your siblings turned out to be HLA-identical, which rules them out as possible donors."

I had already been informed of the mismatch of my brothers and sister as donors. Nevertheless, my throat seized tight again.

Iolanda quickly continued. "Because of this, we have begun a world registry search for potential unrelated donors."

The statistics were dismal. I read that one in three transplant patients never found a donor, either related to them or not. If I were to be fortunate enough to find a match, I would undergo what Iolanda called an allogeneic hematopoietic cell transplantation. In the process, my white blood cells and neutrophils would be completely annihilated. My immune system would be not merely suppressed, like it was in my previous chemotherapy rounds, but eradicated. It would be completely wiped out. I would be at the mercy of any possible infection since I would have no reserves of my own to counteract even the slightest attack on my body. In the event that I did not develop an infection, a donor's new stem cells could be infused into my body. They would engraft into my bone marrow and, some days later, start to make new, healthy blood cells.

"You'll need to undergo a conditioning regimen in the days before the transplant," Iolanda told us. "This consists of high-dose chemotherapy. We will administer myeloablative doses of busulfan in combination with cyclophosphamide. Pretransplant organ functions permitting, of course."

I stared, unblinking, at her.

"The end effect is to administer the most intense chemotherapy treatment possible. The aim is to destroy even the last microscopic leukemic cells that might still linger."

A pause. I felt my heartbeat hammer against my chest wall.

"Explained more graphically," Iolanda said quietly. She lowered her eyes for a moment. "It is a sub-lethal dose of chemotherapy."

She halted, less this time to ponder her next explanations, I think, than to allow me to absorb the impact of this information. I was too afraid to look at Nick. I did not want to see his expression. Iolanda consulted the binder in front of her. She pushed several green sheets of paper across the table towards me. They described the risks, toxicities and complications of a bone marrow transplant.

"Infusing donor cells carries risks. Allergic reactions may occur. There is also a risk of graft failure or graft rejection. We call this graft-versus-host disease, or GVHD. We would give an immunosuppressive medication called tacrolimus to prevent this. However, complications may still emerge. The most common are liver, renal, cardiac and pulmonary damage that could be fatal."

I felt my face blanch. Panicky, disjointed thoughts clamored in my mind. The transplanted cells could, at any given moment, see my body as foreign. They could be rejected. My immune system would be gone. There was the risk of organ failure. I might not even survive the immediate days after the transplant. I felt bile surge up in my throat.

I doubled over and vomited into a paper recycling container near the conference table.

Iolanda gave me a moment. "We are prepared to deal with all possible side effects." Her look was sympathetic as she handed me some tissues from a Kleenex box. "There is no wrong choice. But it is a decision the two of you will have to make."

I reeled. It was a matter of facing death up front by undergoing the transplant, taking my chance. Or I could watch, wait, and linger until the disease relapsed. All of a sudden percentages and graphs seemed ludicrous. From my standpoint there were only two possible outcomes. My chances were 50/50. Either I made it. Or I didn't.

Iolanda handed the consent packet binder to me and told me to think it over after I returned to Alaska. "Don't delay in your decision making," she said squarely, holding my gaze this time.

Leaden, I managed to nod. Nick and I, numb and speechless, turned to walk out.

"Oh!" Iolanda exclaimed behind us, remembering suddenly the sticky note she had placed on my chart. "And Happy Birthday!"

Nick and I looked at each other, dumbfounded. We had forgotten it was the day before my birthday. I would turn forty-three tomorrow.

CHAPTER 32
Chena Ridge Trails

Under the quickly gained daylight of early May in Alaska, the sun rose earlier each morning, its light softer, less angular. The hills around town turned to fuller green. The last remnant ice on the rivers melted. Moose fed on the bottom of bogs, lifting their great antlered heads from the water, mosses trailing. On the forested slopes, bears were stirring out of hibernation dens, heart rates quickening again after their long winter sleep.

On a crisp spring morning, Rebecca, Tara and I went for a long walk along the trails on Chena Ridge. We followed a narrow trail through a forest of white spruce and birch and tamarack, typical of the latitude. The trail dipped into hollows, then climbed again. The land was undeveloped, its trails crisscrossed rough and rooted. Fallen leaves and spruce needles obscured the trail. A breeze swooshed gently. We met no one. We walked in single file. Tara and Rebecca talked back over their shoulders, following landmarks that had guided us on previous walks. A large spruce at the junction of the upper trails, the bee field, the "enchanted" tree, the rusty hay mowing machine, the stile, the "Narnia" lamppost, the potato field.

I followed, too preoccupied with my thoughts to breathe in the scenery. I was living on borrowed time. My bone marrow transplant date was set for June 1. With a trembling hand I had signed the consent forms, then fled to Alaska for my final respite. While the National Marrow Donor Program urgently scanned databases and registries for a possible donor for me, I counted the days before I was due back in Seattle. Time was of the essence, I realized, as I was gambling with every relapse-free day.

Morbidly, I combed through the obituary section of the newspaper each morning, trying to decipher how many of the deceased had died of cancer. Would I, too, become a statistic? I did not know that Tara and

Rebecca had talked about driving to my house to hide the newspapers from me.

"Did you even hear me?" Rebecca was asking, smiling at me.

I surfaced from the fringes of my thoughts. We had reached the open clearing at the meeting of several trails, a large meadow surrounded by the forest. The sun was warm. The tall grasses undulated. Two musk ox, shaggy and pre-historic looking, stood slumbering at the edge of the field.

"The musk ox are out today," Rebecca repeated.

I looked at the tranquil scene in front of me, but everything seemed to exist apart from me. "I can't think of anything but the transplant," I conceded bitterly.

The days since our meeting with Iolanda in Seattle had passed quietly. I regained my appetite, my strength and finally my hair. I slept in my own bed again underneath the slanting eaves, inhaling the comfort of freshly washed sheets. On the weekend, I sat on a camping chair on the sideline of the turf field, snow piles still melting on the edges, where Helen's soccer team had shoveled the field. Huddled in fleece, I watched them play. White and knobby kneed after the long winter, they called to each other, ponytails flying. In the evening I roasted chicken in the oven along with lemon potatoes and sat with my family at the dinner table, prudently grateful to partake.

"I don't know why I can't continue this way," I told my friends. "I feel fine."

We stood and watched the musk ox, stocky and long-haired, as they nuzzled the grasses. Their qiviut, the soft under wool prized for its softness and warmth, had not yet been combed out.

"The way you strode up that last hill, this transplant should be a piece of cake," Tara pointed out after a bit.

"You'll be back in no time," Rebecca nodded her encouragement. "I'd rather miss one summer in order to gain the rest of my summers, don't you think?"

I nodded, bravely, throat tight. We walked back on the trail in silence; musk ox, trail, sunshine forgotten.

In the newspaper, which I retrieved from my mailbox after our walk, I read that the sister of Fairbanks' former mayor, fighting leukemia for seven months, had died at the University of Washington's Medical Center. She had succumbed to complications from a bone marrow transplant.

CHAPTER 33
German Women

Heavy hearted, Nick and I sat at my desk, pondering the stacks of bills that had accumulated: Polar Fuel, AT&T telephone, Water Wagon, Golden Valley Electric. We had reached the credit limit on our bank card. Our savings were vanishing quickly. We had to formulate a plan. Arrangements needed to be made. We had to find long-term housing. The SCCA House, where we previously stayed, was suited only for short-term residents. We would need to use our reserves to pay for my lengthy stay in Seattle, the rent for another apartment, the cost of the transplant that our medical insurance would not cover, airplane tickets.

"Let's think about this carefully," Nick said. "We will need to have caretakers for the time after the transplant. For one hundred days. Roughly three months. That's how long you'll have to stay within the radius of the hospital."

Who would come? Where would the children stay? How could Nick possibly continue working in Fairbanks while I was undergoing a transplant in Seattle? My mind was a tumult.

"Maybe our family members can take turns?" I suggested. "Maybe two weeks at a time?"

With the calendar at hand, we humbly telephoned our families to determine who could come, week after week, to bridge the span of three months. We thought of our extended family members one by one—nieces, siblings, parents—and considered them travelling from Germany and Greece to help us. They all lived far away, across mountains and land and sea.

We were met with deliberation and hesitation.

"It may be a little difficult at that time of year," came one response. "The kids are still in school."

I sat down, abruptly, not expecting this. They were burdened with careers and families. The children's school schedule, their days off work, the distance to travel – all obstacles seemingly too great. I dialed the next number.

"Yes, the last week in June might be possible. Maybe the first week of July. Would that suffice? I'll have to check with my boss at work first." Then, "You would pay for my flights, right?" I hung up, stunned.

Nick picked up the phone and dialed someone on his list.

"That is the time of the wedding," was the response. "We've been busy planning it. But maybe I could come afterwards?"

They were not hurtling themselves to my rescue, coming quickly, armed with comfort. I was overcome with a terrible sadness that stretched wispy and thin. Was I not as important, as worthy a member of the extended family?

"Like cockroaches that scatter in the light," Nick said, blighted. After all the times we had crossed oceans for them, they would not even jump a puddle for us. Crushed, Nick and I looked at each other.

But then, just as we bottomed out, there was a pocket of hope.

"We will come," both my mother and my sister offered at once, no questions asked. I nodded vigorously into the telephone, unable to utter a word past my solidified throat.

"Nick will be with you right after you get discharged from the hospital. I will come for the next three weeks," my mother decided firmly. "Andrea will come for the final three weeks. And then you will go home."

A weight eased inside me. They would take charge. They would come to my aid: prepared, organized, capable. Nick sighed audibly, relieved, pressing my shoulder as he got up. Perhaps it would work out after all. I remained seated, bills and calendar and phone lists still piled up in front of me. My gaze was drawn outdoors.

Images of my childhood in Germany flooded in. It was summertime in Füssen, a town in southern Bavaria, at the foot of the Alps. Trying to keep up with our older brothers, my sister Andrea and I clambered up the forested ridge to build a tree house with wood stolen from the log piles the forestry service had neatly stacked along the *Kobelweg*, a high trail. When our brothers could not lose us in their wake, they put us to work instead. I held logs while Thomas and Michael hammered. Andrea stood *Wache*, sentry, at the bend of the trail, alerting us with a whistle when she saw any passersby. When we returned home at dusk, giddy and excited, we were sworn to silence by the boys. Happily, Andrea and I conceded as long as we were included in our brothers' undertakings.

On other days we rode our rattling bikes over the crooked, cobblestoned roads of the old town. In the *Innenstadt* we pedaled hard after the boys, averting the shouts of cafe owners on the pedestrian *Reichenstrasse*. Sometimes we played hide-and-seek for hours in the underground parking garage next to our apartment complex, disregarding the sign *Zutritt Verboten*: entry forbidden. We combed the telephone booths around the neighborhood, crawling on hands and knees to find dropped ten *pfennig* coins. We wandered around Woolworths, eyeing plastic toy cowboys we were not brave enough to shoplift. On hot days, we swam in the green water of the triple lakes in *Bad Faulenbach*. When we felt more adventurous, we plunged into the icy cold water of the *Alatsee* high up in the mountains, a lake so deep that submarines were tested in its depths during World War II.

When we returned in the evening to the flat on the *Hohenstaufenstrasse* our mother awaited us, eyebrow raised. Andrea and I, giggling, finally went to sleep in the bunkbed we shared. We were accomplices in childhood antics. She was my confidante, my closest friend. And night always descended gently.

My mother, contrary to German punctiliousness, often turned a blind eye. She let us children romp around but managed to keep us in stride at the same time. Sternly, she sat us all down at the kitchen table to admonish us when complaints surfaced. The older couple from the apartment below had grumbled about the noise level, our trampling feet, the screech of the wooden chair legs as we pushed away from the kitchen table. After reprimanding us, however, my mother organized a stroll into town to buy ice cream from the Italian *Dolomiti* cafe.

She abided by our regimented, rule-following German neighbors, apologizing for our pranks beneath a tirade from onlooking neighboring balconies. We had run barefoot across the manicured lawn. It was for aesthetic viewing, not romping, the neighbors scolded. When Michael, little at the time, picked roses from the communal flowerbed, my mother tried to explain that he could not, possibly, distinguish cultivated roses from wild dandelions. When Andrea and I hung up the laundry on the outdoor rotary drying umbrella we pegged up undergarments, unshielded, on the outermost line. The lady that lived on the bottom floor of our apartment block was horrified when she looked out of her window directly at the flapping bras and knickers. Again, my mother shrugged. She could not see what difference it made whether the underwear dried in front of or behind the pillowcases. When we ran, loud and boisterous, down the echoing stairwell during the midday rest time, my mother diffused the harum-scarum and the irritated neighbors by taking us to play mini golf in *Bad Faulenbach* instead.

On weekends, to imbue some culture into us, she and my father organized field trips to surrounding churches. We marched through the austere looking abbey in *Steingaden*, the monastery of Ettal where monks still brewed beer, and the rococo *Wieskirche* while our father explained architectural details to us. We were fascinated with the castles of Ludwig II of Bavaria, *Neuschwanstein* and *Hohenschwangau* and *Linderhof*. The king had emptied the coffers of Bavaria to build the castles, then died mysteriously while swimming in a lake.

While we didn't all fit into the car for the outings, my mother told us to pile in anyway. We sat on each other's laps, unbuckled, and ducked low when we caught sight of a police car. Rules and regulations sometimes had to be bent a little, my mother said, winking at us. Life did not need to be that complicated.

A feeling of ease spread through me. My mother and my sister would come to Seattle. Together, we would handle what was to come. After all, we came from a strong lineage of German women. Weren't we descendants of the *Trümmerfrauen*, the "women of the rubble" who took care of the wounded, salvaged belongings, and cleared away the rubble and ruin of World War II? Surely, we would manage to get through the debris a bone marrow transplant would leave behind in its aftermath, pick up the pieces, and move on?

Two days later I left for Seattle. Minutes before my departure, I got a message from the National Marrow Donor Program. A suitable donor for my bone marrow transplant had been found. A woman. Twenty-one years of age. From Germany.

CHAPTER 34
Seattle Outings

"You'll be able to see the fireworks over Lake Union on the 4th of July."

The landlady let the children and me into the apartment. Its windows looked north. Across the din and noise of four lanes of traffic on Fairview Avenue, we could see the lake in the distance.

Yanni and Helen beamed. In Alaska, Independence Day fireworks were always lost on us. The sun did not set in the summer and the nights never darkened enough to see sparklers and rockets burst colorfully in the sky. Here, finally, was their chance to see a real fireworks display.

The children were my first caretakers. Nick and I decided that they should accompany me to Seattle while I underwent my pre-transplant conditioning. I still felt healthy and strong. Nick would continue working in Alaska until the days just before my transplant. Then he would take over.

Yanni and Helen ran off immediately to explore the rooms of the apartment, excited about starting their summer holiday in the big city. The corner apartment was on the fifth floor of the Pete Gross House. It was a tall building with a blue and yellow façade, a deserted rooftop garden scattered with pigeon droppings, and, much to the delight of the children, a garbage chute that trash could clatter down.

"The house was named after Pete Gross," the landlady explained to us. "You know, the commentator of the Seahawks? He battled cancer for years and his family wanted people undergoing treatment away from home to have a comfortable place to recuperate."

The occupants of the house lived in isolation, closed off. Doors were decorated with colorful paper flowers onto which schoolchildren had written the message: "Hope grows." The house's residents stayed long-term, extending stays over months at a time. In seclusion after transplants, they were slowly rebuilding their immune systems. Aside from the rumbling of a dryer in someone's apartment, the house was silent. No television noise, no voices, no sounds of everyday living. It was a house for the seriously ill.

"The shuttle bus can take you to the clinic if you need transportation," the landlady continued, walking into the living room and adjoining kitchen. "And it goes to Safeway twice a day if you need groceries."

I looked around the apartment. It was situated in a corner of the building, facing the distant lake to the north and another apartment complex across the street to the east. The living room was small but sufficient. A greenish-grey fabric couch and low coffee table faced a TV cabinet set in a corner of the room. The carpet, faded mauve, looked worn near the balcony door.

A kitchenette separated itself by means of a Formica countertop from a round wooden dining table. The kitchen was old but clean. Utensils and knives were separated into trays labeled "cooking" and "eating." There were cutting boards for "meat," others for "vegetables." Antiseptic dish washing solution and Clorox containers stood on the countertop. Paper towels hung in a roll under the cabinet. A chart hung on the wall delineating foods deemed safe to eat while immunocompromised. Nothing undercooked was allowed. No smoked salmon, Sushi, tofu. No sunny side up or over easy eggs. No unpasteurized dairy and cheese. No probiotic yoghurt. Reheated food should reach 165°F before eating. Fruits and vegetables should be scrubbed and peeled before eating. Bottled water was preferable to water from the faucet.

A tiny balcony, just wide enough to accommodate two plastic chairs, overlooked Minor Avenue. Yanni and Helen peered over the railing, observing the street activity below. I went to stand beside them and felt the proximity of the apartment buildings across the street, the density of urban living. I missed Alaska already.

After the landlady left, I felt no desire to unpack our suitcases or to orient ourselves in our new abode. All of a sudden, the small rooms of the apartment felt constricting and airless. I wanted to be outdoors, some place green and unrestrained and unshackled.

"Shall we go to the zoo?" I asked the children, unexpectedly.

They both blinked at me. I was already pulling out my cell phone, googling the number for Seattle Yellow Cab.

At Woodland Park Zoo, we stood in front of the northern trail exhibit and spotted the twin grizzly bears slumbering in the shade of a large pine. Both Yanni and Helen fell silent. The exhibit was well adapted to the bears' needs, with a stream running through it, a deep pool in which they could fish for trout and space to wander. Trees and rocky boulders dotted a sunny hillside.

"Are they ever let out?" Helen asked, her hands pressing against the Plexiglass that separated us from them.

"That one is called Denali," Yanni commented, reading the signage. "Like our mountain at home."

Their experience of bears in Alaska was of a different nature. Once, on a summer camping trip to Brushkana Creek, we encountered a large brown bear in the wild. We spent a long weekend at the creek, picking blueberries, wading in the icy current as it tripped over polished river stones, sitting on camping chairs under the midnight sun. On Sunday evening, the children and I packed our sleeping bags and tents into the pickup truck to drive back to Fairbanks. Yanni and Helen, tired after a long weekend outdoors, pulled out Nintendos to play Mario Kart.

Not long after we started driving down the Denali Highway—a rutted, potholed, gravel road—an enormous brown bear lumbered out from the willows that bordered the road. I came to an abrupt stop, mere feet away from him. We were close enough to make out the characteristic hump on his shoulder, his cinnamon hide and the flicker of his eye.

"A grizzly!" I called out to the children. They glanced up promptly, distracted from their games. We stared at the great creature in awe. He stood up on his powerful hind legs, his height towering to get a closer look at us. We held our breath. Then he loped down the gravel road for a distance, nimble footed despite his size, before turning and disappearing into the willow bushes again. A slight rustling of the leaves covered the gap in the willows. Any sign of the bear was instantly gone. The children turned their attention back to their games. I, however, sat for some moments in the golden dusk and looked at the spot in the billowing bushes where the bear had vanished. What a privilege it was to have encountered him on his land.

Around us in the zoo, a group of schoolchildren on a field trip gathered noisily. Despite their teacher's attempt at hushing them, they cackled and shouted and rapped against the Plexiglass. In the distance, the bear named Denali raised his head and slowly retreated out of sight behind some boulders. Was he content?

I could thwart the imminence of ailment and hospitals and impairment by organizing excursions with my children and evading the circumstances that had brought me to Seattle in the first place. I, too, could reach an agreement with my confinement. Perhaps I could even feel at ease within the yoke of my reality. The bear lived in the zoo like I would in the apartment. Suspended in a space that was neither home nor wild, neither bound nor free, always wondering whether, one day, we would be free of our restriction.

We walked slowly back through the animal exhibits to the front entrance of the zoo. Yanni and Helen took only fleeting glances at the giraffes in the savanna, who earlier they had excitedly hand fed acacia leaves to. They hardly noticed the hippopotamus, across a moat from us, as she lounged on a muddy bank near the water. I felt their downcast demeanors without even looking at them. The thought of returning to the small apartment in the city seemed stifling.

"Let's go to the movies," I suggested to them.

They brightened immediately. I hailed a cab. We had hardly clambered in when Helen excitedly gushed out to the cab driver: "Mom's taking us to see a movie! It's as though she isn't even sick."

The cab driver, a dark skinned, bearded man who spoke with the lilt of an Indian accent smiled at her exuberance, then rested his glance on me in the rearview mirror. His look registered confusion.

"I'm feeling fine," I told him finally.

I did not want to go into the details. I turned to look out of the window, spirits dampened. He dropped us on Pine Street, near the Pacific Place mall.

"Be well," he told me quietly with a slight bow when I handed him a tip.

I managed to smile, though I felt a surge of angst build up again. I was just going to a movie with my children. When had that become such a privilege in life? I quickly steered the children towards the mall entrance.

On the fifth floor of the mall, we peered at posters advertising movies.

"Oh please, Mom," Yanni begged, pointing at one. "Can we see The Dictator? It will be funny."

Distracted, still thinking about the comment of the cab driver, I paid for the tickets. The girl at the ticket office sported pink hair and a nose ring. She eyed Helen.

"How old is she?" she asked. "The movie may not be age appropriate for her."

I bristled, irrationally, spurned on my increasingly foul mood.

"She's nine," I challenged her. "I'm her mother! And I have cancer!"

I realized, soon into the movie, that the ticket girl had been correct in her assessment. Aladeen, the dictator, spewed crude sexist and anti-Semitic comments. Sexually explicit scenes made both children squirm uncomfortably. I wasn't even able to laugh at the obvious parody the movie was making out of the dictator and his Republic of Wadiya. A heaviness settled itself over me, pregnant with a sense of doom. I whispered to Helen, who was constantly tugging on my sleeve, that I would explain the details of the movie later. I was glad we had chosen a matinee showing. The darkened theater was empty save for a handful of watchers. At least I was spared any more disapproving looks.

Afterwards, as we waited on the curb for a taxi, I spotted an AT&T store across the road. Impulsively I entered, with the children trailing behind.

"I would like two cell phones," I told the clerk, "One for each of them."

Yanni and Helen gaped while I ignored the salesman's questioning look.

It took just an instant for me to discard my carefully constructed philosophy on the negative impact of cell phone technology and social media on children. Nowadays young people had no social skills anymore, I always maintained. No eye contact, no hand shaking, no interactive communication. It all resulted, in my opinion, from their reliance on texting and screens. They could not even write properly anymore. Punctuation was discarded, grammar amiss, phrase eloquence absent. Cell phones held all power. They autocorrected texts, suggested synonyms and even translated their missives into different languages. I had planned on refraining from buying Yanni and Helen cell phones for as long as possible. Until now.

"Just a basic plan," I told the clerk. "I want the kids to be able to reach me at all times." As though a telephone could somehow keep us all connected, could span any distance between us and could reassure them that I would always be there to answer on the other end.

On our return to the apartment, while the children excitedly sorted out their new phones, I stood on the tiny balcony. The rain had ceased and left behind black asphalt that glittered in the lights of the cars below. I inhaled the air, but my breath drew shallow. No excursion, no outing, and no cell phone could stall the ticking of the clock.

CHAPTER 35
Anniversary Chemo

"You'll be able to administer the chemo yourself, initially, as an outpatient," Dr. Dunahew explained radiantly, as though she had just presented me with a grand prize.

She was the attending doctor of the "Lime Team," the transplant team I was assigned to. I had met her for the first time only a few minutes earlier. Tall and seasoned, with short blond hair turning grey at the temples, she appeared well versed in the business of transplants. I sensed that she had accompanied many patients through the procedure, following meticulous protocol, a strictly devised plan. Aside from Dr. Dunahew, the Lime Team consisted of a registered nurse, a nutritionist, a scheduler and a social worker. Dr. Dunahew handed me a sheet with their contact information, office phones, cell phones. All would work diligently to keep me safe, she told me. They were available to me at all times.

We sat in a conference room at the clinic, windows overlooking a fantastically sunny day in Seattle. Lake Union sparkled. Yachts swiveled gently at their moorings off lakeside piers. Waiters at waterfront restaurants were opening umbrellas at patio tables, setting places for lunch.

I left the children in the apartment. For the past three weeks, they had taken their role as my caretaker earnestly, keeping track of my appointments on the kitchen wall calendar, alerting me when it was time to go. I followed the countdown fastidiously.

Scans evaluated my pre-transplant organ functions. A pulmonary function test determined the capacity of my lungs. A dental appointment assessed the condition of my teeth and gums. Yanni and Helen accompanied me to all appointments, legs dangling from waiting room chairs, leafing through magazines.

In a food safety and post-transplant care class they sat next to me, thoughtful and attentive. When the nurse nutritionist summarized the day's session, asking questions about foods that were to be avoided and how to sterilize the environment I lived in, both raised their hands eagerly.

"Why should we not keep fish in an aquarium while we are recuperating from the transplant?"

"Because bacteria can grow in the fish tank water," Yanni offered at once.

"Is it alright to have dogs and cats in the house?" the nurse continued.

"Yes," Helen responded. "But it's not okay to pick up the dog poop or clean the litter box."

"How about gardening?"

"Watering plants is alright, but digging in the dirt is not," Yanni answered.

The rest of the class, comprised of anxious, note-taking caregivers and subdued, pre-transplant patients, had to smile at them.

But now, they were packing their belongings into suitcases. They were leaving on an afternoon flight to Germany, to stay with my family while I underwent the transplant. After much deliberation, balking and reluctant, I agreed with Nick. It would be easier to have relatives take care of them this summer. A sense of dread overcame me. The children were leaving. The transplant was beginning.

I turned to listen to Dr. Dunahew again.

"You won't even need to be in the hospital until a day or two before your transplant." A huge smile creased her elongated face.

She shuffled through her folder and gave me a sheet of paper on which she had outlined a timeline, a chronology of my life to come. The days of the pre-transplant conditioning were counted in negative numbers: -3, -2, -1. My transplant day, Day 0, was set for June 1. Then began the positive days: +1, +2, +3. If, on Day 100, all went well, I would return home.

We had approached Day -7. With one week to go, I was to start my outpatient chemotherapy. Dr. Dunahew pushed a pill container across the table. Capsuled, tiny blue pills: chemotherapy, toxic, annihilating.

"You will take Busulfan in pill form, orally, every six hours, for a total of 16 doses, starting tomorrow, May 25. You'll be admitted to the hospital for the final conditioning of Cytoxan, on May 29 and 30. Then you get one day of rest, on May 31, before the transplant, on June 1."

I looked at the pills. I was to administer them into my body myself. I would be the instrument of my body's break down, its weakening, its ruin. And then, when I had caused its plummet from health, I would be admitted into the hospital for even more destruction. Precisely on May 29, the day that marked my wedding anniversary. Instead of going to a candlelit dinner with my husband, where we could smile and think back on our eighteen years of marriage, I would check myself into the transplant floor of the hospital. In some dim functioning rationale of my terrified mind, I wondered whether the course of events, thus outlined, were more frightening than the transplant itself. To know what was to come, to possibly be an agent in my own demise, to agree to proceed towards disaster when the screeching in my head said no, no, no!

With the pills in my jeans pocket, I walked leadenly back to the apartment. The neighborhood looked the same. The paved streets, the blocky apartment buildings, the trees that grew at regular intervals along the sidewalk all looked as they had when I walked to the clinic earlier. People hurried past, not casting a glance at me. On the corner of Mercer and Minor, orange construction fencing forced me to cross to the other sidewalk. The worker I encountered this morning was still jackhammering at a widening crack in the road. Pipes lay alongside. I stepped over these and trudged on.

In the forty-five minutes since my appointment everything had changed. I would start swallowing the pills tomorrow. Dr. Dunahew judged that the benefit of taking Busulfan, a medication that could cause serious side effects, was greater than the risks. I was cast into the role of an undertaker now, orchestrating my own downfall.

When I returned to the apartment, I sat down on the edge of Helen's bed, between scattered clothes and books and board games.

"Should I take everything, Mom?" Helen asked. Her suitcase bulged. "We'll be there for a long time, right?"

I swallowed. "Take anything you want," I told her quietly.

Contrary to my usual habit of packing lightly, I did not criticize her untidy cramming. Instead of reaching over to fold her sweatshirt more carefully, to tuck away her toothbrush and comb into a toiletry bag or to slide a book into the bag, I just sat and watched her chestnut hair fall over her forehead, her slender arms, her long, crossed legs. When had the years overtaken us so? I still felt her closeness when I held her as a baby, remembering how she reached up, pacifier in mouth, to touch the softness of my hair or my eyebrow.

When we piled into the taxi that would take us to the airport, I told myself that I had to hold out for just a little longer still, to maintain my brazen facade. My hand trembled when we stood at Lufthansa's check-in counter as I signed the unaccompanied minor consent form. A wash of doubt flooded me. I summoned every bit of strength I could to conceal the faltering iron constitution I had tried to fortify myself with.

"How exciting!" I smiled at them, adjusting the strap on Helen's backpack. "You'll be able to spend the summer with Jason and Joanna and Cedric and Fiona in Munich. What fun you'll have!"

Helen squirmed impatiently, eyes shining, clutching her boarding pass. She had always gotten on well with her German cousins.

Yanni looked at me, his face unguarded. "You'll be all better when we get back, right, Mom?"

The air felt thick, difficult to breathe. I nodded at him as I pulled him and his sister close to hide the tears that were welling. I inhaled their scent, committing them to my deepest core. Both stood patiently, knowing my embrace would not last forever, eager for the flight attendant to accompany them down to the airplane. Helen tripped along in her excitement. Yanni stepped more sedately. Just before the bend in the jetway, they both looked back and smiled at me, waving. I lifted my hand in response, quivering, then turned quickly, lest they see me crumble. The day had pulverized me.

CHAPTER 36
The Bone Cave

"What if the cells don't arrive in time?" I asked Ruth, grabbing her hand.

A new panic gripped me, a fear I had not thought of before. My donor's stem cells were coming across an ocean and a continent. What if the airplane they were transported on was cancelled? What if weather related concerns delayed their arrival? I had reached a point of no return, my own immune system destroyed, a new one not yet developed.

"Do you remember when 9/11 brought all air traffic to a standstill above America?" Ruth soothed in her usual calm manner. "Stem cell recipients were still able to get their donor cells. Airplanes were diverted to Canada. Cells were transported here on trucks. Your cells will arrive, don't worry."

I breathed again.

The room looked no different than the rooms I was housed in before during my previous chemotherapy rounds. Ruth still looked the same, with her bright scrubs and her generous smile. The hospital room was sterile white, with starched sheets on the bed, double pillows stacked. Paneled against the wall above the bed were oxygen valves, a Purell container, outlets painted yellow and green, a conspicuous "code blue" button. A beige curtain could be drawn to conceal the room from the open hallway.

But it was different this time. I had been admitted into the "bone cave."

Years ago, when Nick solidified his medical training at the Ohio State University Medical Center, he attended to complex medical cases: trauma victims airlifted from accident sites, complicated referrals from other hospitals, patients with multiple medical conditions, chronic illnesses with unexplained symptoms. None, he told me, were as difficult as the patients in what the medical students nicknamed the "bone cave." It was the floor dedicated to bone marrow transplants patients. Horrors happened there. Admission to the "bone cave" resulted, almost always, in a devastating outcome. Patients lay confined, bald and ghostly, in screened off rooms. Only medical teams and essential visitors were allowed, to minimize the risk of infecting bodies with non-existent immune systems. There was a hush on the floor, punctuated only by the beeping of machines, a stillness surrounding patients too ill to converse. Medical students emerged, scrubbed and masked, from the isolated and disinfected rooms. Humbled, they breathed in deep, grateful gulps of air outside the hospital when their shift ended. Never, in those years, would Nick ever have imagined that his own wife would be admitted to a "bone cave."

I was reunited with the nurses from before, a tiny consolation in the wrack of my present circumstance. Ruth and Steven and Blayne and Kendra. They sustained me, adjusting medications, changing bedding, offering kind words. Long after Dr. Dunahew and her team left, they sat with me in the darkness when I was too frightened to close my eyes.

The evening before my transplant, I found no sleep. Night fell, black and sinister. The floor was quiet. In the rooms next to mine, down the hall, patients were fighting for their lives through the dark hours. Perhaps dawn would bring with it another loss in the night, a surrender to a battle valiantly fought, the sacrifice of someone's life.

I thought of my donor. She would have donated her stem cells just a day or two ago, so they could be frozen in a cryo-preservative and transported across the ocean. What had prompted her to selflessly give her cells, with no monetary compensation, with no promise that she might even be able to help the recipient of her cells? What frame of mind and heart would allow her to burden herself in this way, to travel distances to a hospital or clinic to become my marrow donor? Had she received stimulating growth hormone injections, aching in her bones for days afterwards, to boost the white blood cells in her blood stream? What method would she have chosen to donate her stem cells? Had she undergone the process of having a needle inserted into her hipbone to extract cells directly from her bone marrow? This was painful, as I knew very well from several bone marrow biopsies I had endured, but the amount of stem cells would be concentrated. Alternatively, she might have opted for an intravenous draw from her arm, which would extract peripheral blood stem cells. Though this method would be less painful for her, the sparseness of stem cells in the bloodstream might have resulted in an insufficient harvest, a failed donation. Would she have persevered after an unsuccessful first attempt? What thoughts would have crossed her mind, as she was prodded with needles, about this decision of hers to help an unknown stranger a world away?

The cells arrived in the small hours of the morning, in a transfusion bag not unlike the ones that had hung from my IV pole so many times in the past months. Ruth, followed by Kendra, switched on the overhead lights. I blinked in the glare. With an air of proprietorship, Ruth carried the bag over to me and slipped it over the hook on my IV pole. She would be the one administering my donor's stem cells to me.

"The cells are only viable for twenty-four hours," she told me. "That is why we have to do this in the middle of the night."

Ruth read off my demographic information to Kendra, spelling out the contents of the transfusion bag to her. I listened, groggy with medication and lack of sleep, to their system of checks and balances. Even though the cells' infusion was urgent, both nurses were calm, quietly taking my blood pressure, then my temperature.

I watched the red liquid trickle slowly down the long, clear tube into my chest. For weeks I had anticipated the day when I would receive my donor's cells, when my future became a possibility again.

It was my turn. I held my breath, urging the new cells to take to my body. They would develop along three different lineages – platelets and red blood cells and white blood cells – sensing, amazingly, how to differentiate into the cells that were deficient in my body, knowing when to stop replicating, adjusting to the work the annihilated diseased cells had left behind for them. My donor's cells would develop into the same immune system that my body's disease had destroyed. They were fighting a war with the same weapons that had destroyed them in the first place like the Inuit people on the Arctic coast, who built igloos, their means of shelter and survival, with the very snow they sought to protect themselves from.

I looked at the bag hanging overhead. That was it. The transplant. It was somewhat anticlimactic. From its look, the only difference between this event in the middle of the night and other transfusions in the past was the knowledge that this bag contained stem cells that had come from my donor. And a card signed by the nurses and staff of the seventh floor. Kendra left it on my bedside table. It read "Happy Cell Day."

A rush of blood in my ears drowned out the sounds of Ruth and Kendra talking. It was another beginning. Another birthday. A second chance granted. A tingling spread though my stomach, flowed into my arms, my fingertips, down my calves to my toes. I could not be sure that the cells would take to my body. Their bare possibility, however, sent tendrils of hope through me.

CHAPTER 37
The Parenthesis

I felt Nick's presence even when my eyes could not focus properly on his features. His head was close to me, lying on the side of the bed. He had fallen asleep sitting on the chair next to me. I wanted to whisper to him, but my lips were cracked and dry. My arm was too heavy to lift. I was unable to run my fingers through his hair.

The high chemotherapy dose left me weak and hovering in a drifting world, my vision cloudy and blurred. For the past few days, I tried to find anchor in the fuzzy shapes of the nurses and Nick next to my bed.

I couldn't eat. I could barely drink a sip of water. The pain in my abdomen was severe. Even liquids racked my raw esophagus and stomach. Ruth and Steven set up a Total Parenteral Nutrition machine next to my bed. It fed liquid nutrition directly into my veins through a tube. Anti-nausea medication and pain relievers only eased my discomfort temporarily.

Sometimes my heart raced, pounding furiously. More often, I was overcome by a fatigue that settled heavily upon me. My head was bald again, itchy to my touch. My muscles atrophied, slumped and thin. My skin looked sallow and flaky. Once, an angry rash developed on my chest and neck, which Dr. Dunahew biopsied immediately but which turned out negative for graft-versus-host disease, a manifestation of cell rejection. The nurses watched constantly for signs of fever, for hives and chills, for changes in my blood pressure or shortness of breath.

It was a time of hyper vigilance and merciful sleep. Nick floated by my bed. I sometimes felt the warmth of his hand on mine. Often, I slept through the nurses' ministrations, willing my body to do the work now, to take over what my mind could not control anymore. I hung vulnerably, in a space between life and death, pendant between countries. My past was slipping. My future was a question. I acquiesced. I could no longer fend off the inevitable. I could not fight against my fate any more than I could stride against an incoming tide. In some sense, my struggle was over.

There were telephone calls during that time, jumbled and nebulous to me. Nick answered them.

"People are praying up and down coastlines, from Alaska to Washington, across oceans, in Germany and in Greece," he told me, his smile gentle.

Sometimes I spoke to the caller.

"*Seelisch glaube ich, dass du es schaffen wirst*," Thomas, my older brother, said quietly to me. *In my soul, I believe you will make it.* I listened to him, as he recounted details of Yanni's and Helen's day in his home, assuring me that they were safe, willing me to get well so they could return. I blinked back tears because he was a brother I had always counted on, full of reassurances that I could not grasp anymore.

Günther, my father, was a whisper on the telephone. He himself was frail, recuperating still from his own surgery.

"*Das schaffen wir,*" he said in the voice that echoed throughout my childhood, one I knew to trust. *We will get through this.*

I pictured him, a gentle man who always thought of others first, whose actions were directed towards our wellbeing even at his own expense. Never did he question hardship and misfortune. I remembered a quote he abided by always: "A light always shines brightest in utter darkness."

"There is a reason for everything," he said softly to me just before hanging up. I yearned for his steadfastness.

Michael, my younger brother, was on a journalistic assignment in Pakistan. He played his flute for me over the telephone. It was a doleful melody, quivering with vibrato, notes that reached me across the world. Unable to speak the words he wanted to utter, he played for me instead. Emotion surged in my throat and, suddenly, I couldn't speak either. I listened for a long time, eventually falling asleep with the telephone still held to my ear.

Most of all I clung to my son Yanni's words, the sound of his voice clear and certain over many miles of ocean and land.

"One day, Mom, you'll be writing your own survivor story."

CHAPTER 38
Cancer Quilts

Day after day, Ruth recorded zeroes in the boxes on a chart she pinned to the bulletin board. My blood counts: white blood cells, neutrophils, hematocrit, platelets. I stared at the ovals she drew. The soldiers of my circulatory system: besieged, pummeled, defeated. My immune system was eradicated. Completely gone.

But then, nine long days after my donor's stem cells infusion, Ruth walked into the room one morning and, with the twitch of a smile, recorded in the white blood cell box a number. It was only a fraction of a number: 0.12. A number still measuring hugely short of where white blood cells normally range, somewhere between 4.3 and 10.0 thousand. To me, however, it was a number at once diminutive and grand. It was a confirmation.

I looked at Ruth, wide-eyed. I raised an eyebrow, questioning.

"Does this mean…?" I began.

She broke out into a huge smile, nodding. "It does indeed!" she exploded happily.

My donor's stem cells had engrafted. I smiled back. It had really happened.

Encouraged, I mustered enough strength to get out of my bed, to walk down the long hospital corridor in quiet celebration of the first milestone of my bone marrow transplant.

I looked at the signs that hung outside the patients' rooms. A patient's last name, a doctor's last name, a defining condition. Patients were labeled: hematology, oncology, transplant. Humbly, I registered that it was the names on the transplant patients' rooms that changed most frequently. Had their cells not engrafted? I could not be sure of their fate exactly. Had they been discharged from the hospital, furloughing from life for some time in a setting of recovery? Or had they surrendered to their illness altogether?

I hobbled, as quickly as I could, to the safety of my room again.

"Did you know that Jose Carreras, the opera tenor, underwent his transplant here?" Nick said chattily when I returned to the room. "He now gives benefit concerts in Seattle every year to raise funds for leukemia research."

I didn't know that. I sat down on the bed.

"And you know who else?" Nick continued, helping me prop myself up on the pillows and pulling the bed sheet over my legs. "Susan Butcher, the famous sled dog musher who won the Iditarod Race in Alaska four times." Casting his glance downwards, he quietly added, "She didn't make it, though."

They were celebrities: important people onto whom the world casts an eye. Cancer shows neither discrimination nor favoritism. I was among their ranks now. The slate was drawn clean. Whatever lives we had chosen to live pre-cancer—decisions made, stakes risked, comforts indulged in—were all reduced to the same level now. The outcome was a balanced wager. I asked myself who or what allowed us to either live or die. There was no bargaining here, as we stood humbled and meek at the bottom rung of life's ladder. There was only the will to continue. Or not.

A knock came from the door. Two older women, masked and gowned, pushed a cart into my room. On it, tidily stacked, were brightly colored and meticulously stitched quilts.

"We wanted to offer you a quilt," one of the ladies said. Her eyes loomed large and kind over her blue facemask, magnified and swimming behind the thick lenses of her glasses. "They were stitched by volunteers in the community to support patients like you."

I ran my fingers across the fabric of the quilt on the top of the pile. Squares of solid pink and red patchwork alternated with floral designs. The backside was a children book's illustration: a boy and girl gardening, wheelbarrow and basket strewn with picked flowers, a small Scottie dog bounding. I thought of Helen. She would have loved it. I smiled at the lady and her companion and draped the quilt across my legs. It felt soft and comforting.

"Thank you," I told them as they wheeled their cart out of the room again.

I fingered the fabric and gazed at the labor-intensive work that had gone into its creation. It attested to the passage of time. Possibly, the length of time needed to finish a quilt amounted to that needed for cancer treatment. What experiences of the quilter had informed the selection of colors, the association of stories, the choice of patterns? Had they, too, experienced cancer in their family, wishing now to share their commonality with patients like me? And other patients on the floor, who I had never laid eyes on, who were also touching quilts in their isolated rooms. All connected, hemstitched together in the fabric of cancer.

That afternoon, I ventured out of my room again for a short walk on my own. Near the windows overlooking Lake Washington, I stopped to catch my breath and to remind myself of the world outside.

Today a man stood there, in dressing gown and slippers, a fellow patient. His complexion was white, his walk shaky and deliberate, his eyes dark and hollow. He smiled at me when I approached. I dallied. It was not often I saw another patient out in the hallway.

"Lymphoma?" he asked frankly, as a means of starting the conversation.

"Leukemia," I answered.

In our world, there was no need to skirt reality.

"Was your transplant autologous?" he asked.

"Allogeneic," I said.

He looked out the window for a moment. "Mine was autologous."

He was able to use his own stem cells for the transplant, a procedure devoid of the risks of graft-versus-host disease, perhaps a measure easier than mine.

"I relapsed though," he continued. "I had to have a second transplant."

I swallowed hard.

"Do you have kids?" he changed the subject.

"Two," I answered, relieved, always happy to talk about Yanni and Helen. "They are nine and eleven. You?"

"My son is twenty-five," he told me. "He lives here in Seattle. Works for Boeing."

For some time, we just stood side by side, silently looking out over the distant water.

"If I relapse again," he told me after a while, quietly and definitively, "I am going to end treatment. My son is older now. He can manage on his own."

I turned to look at him. I had no words.

He shuffled off but turned a few steps later towards me again.

"You, however, need to keep on fighting," his smile was sad. "If only for your young kids."

I stood for a long while after he left, looking out at the misty day over the distant water. It was difficult to distinguish the horizon in the haze. Water and sky segued into each other in their variegated greyness.

Is living on or letting go the more chivalrous thing to do?

CHAPTER 39
The Guardian Tree

When we built our house in Alaska, high up on Chena Ridge, our construction crew eyed the forested slope that was our land.

"We will need to remove the trees," the job manager told us, "In order to make space for the foundation for the house."

It was a difficult terrain, steep and wooded. The widened trail that was destined to become a driveway curved through birch and cottonwood, descending sharply to where we all stood, on a plateau, surveying the land.

"Can we not just take down what is absolutely necessary?" I asked.

Despite their efforts to accommodate me, by the end of the week most of the trees were felled, crisscrossed across the slope of the hill, revealing the struggle and scars of the years in their exposed trunks and turned-up tree roots. I was saddened at the sight. A Native American proverb crossed my mind: "We do not inherit the land from our ancestors, we borrow it from our children."

On the periphery of the cleared land the aspens still grew thick, root systems connected underground, spreading and cloning. They wavered in the breeze, their flattened leaves twitching and quavering. I smiled, uplifted. Their rustling leaves made music, a tree that you could find with your ears.

Directly in front of the leveled area that would serve as the foundation of our house, a single white spruce remained. It was not a perfect specimen. Its symmetry was lacking and its upper branches straggly. But it stood tall against the valley, guarding what would become our home. To this single tree was passed on the stewardship of the felled land.

Hermann Hesse, the German poet and novelist, wrote that one should listen silently and carefully to trees for a long time in order for them to reveal their core, their meaning. Listening was not so much a matter of escaping from one's suffering, he wrote, though it may have seemed so, given the soothing effect of the sound of the leaves. Instead, it was a longing for home, for stability. My strength is trust, a tree says. And once we have learned to listen to trees, they would always lead us home.

I thought about our "guardian tree" often in the days after my transplant, but especially after my encounter with the other transplant patient in the hospital hallway. In my mind I conjured the spruce tree's sway in front of our house, bearing snow in the winter, providing a stronghold for the first chickadees of the spring on its highest branches. I thought I could hear its whisper in my ear.

CHAPTER 40
Bedtime Story

On a midsummer day, three weeks later, Nick pushed me out of the hospital in a wheelchair. We waited for a taxi to pull up onto the semicircular driveway in front of the hospital. I felt the warmth of the sun spread slowly across my face and arms. The air smelled of pines that grew on the university campus across Pacific Avenue. And of the mulched flowerbeds—dahlias and marigolds and lilies—beside me. A gentle breeze stirred. Without warning, tears started streaming down my cheeks, silent and unstoppable. Nick placed his hand on my shoulder, pressing gently. He did not try to console me. Gratitude ached in my chest.

In our apartment, my mother waited. She had arrived from Germany, for a second time, to care for me. This time I did not weep into her chest or cling to her embrace like I had when she came to me the first time, nine long months ago, shortly after my diagnosis.

"I've lost my hair again," I told her, without preamble, in greeting.

My mother smiled sadly, touching a hand to my cheek, saying nothing. Numbed after the past months, we found the need for fewer and fewer words. We were beyond embraces and tears. We were changed persons, at once grateful and harrowed. Our havoc had been too raw, hers as mother, mine as her child. I was sure that my mother often collided with reason, questioning constantly. To first be granted a child, whom she had raised carefully and lovingly throughout childhood years, only to watch her torture when she was at her prime, helpless in the face of illness and terror. It amounted to the ultimate assault upon a mother.

That evening, my mother busied herself in the kitchen and made *Pfannekuchen*, German pancakes that she spread with applesauce and sugar. The three of us, Nick and my mother and I, sat at the wooden table that so many cancer patients had sat at before us. We quietly ate them for dinner. I had returned, we all silently thought. Others had not been so fortunate. I wanted to make sense of it all, to reconcile the anguish of the past months into a justification, an explanation. I felt so tired then, knowing that there would be no rationale genuine enough to pardon that type of trauma.

When my mother helped me to bed and pulled my pajama top over my thin shoulders, careful not to disturb the port lines still embedded in my chest, I asked her to tell me a story. I wanted the world to fall away.

"Tell me about your first post, when you first went abroad." I leaned back into my pillows like a child readying herself for a bedtime story. I would never tire of it, even though I had heard it recounted multiple times.

"We went to Poona, in western India," my mother told me, sitting down on the edge of the bed. "It was a two-and-a-half-hour train ride from Bombay. When we got assigned the post, I had to look it up on an atlas."

My parents left Germany for a series of assignments, all in different countries, moving every three or five or seven years. My father worked as the director of the Goethe Institute, a German cultural entity dedicated to the exchange of culture and language abroad. With four young children in tow, my parents moved from country to country -- India, Indonesia, Chile, Argentina, Egypt. They embraced new assignments, absorbing unfamiliar customs and languages. They established their abode in foreign lands.

They arrived in India in June of 1965, just in time for the southwest monsoon that brought heavy downpours. The thermometer read 980 F, making their clothes cling damply to their skin. They stood, in the general chaos that was Victoria Station. Clutching my brother Thomas, a baby of eight months, they took in their surroundings in a somewhat bewildered manner. A mass of humanity surrounded them. Porters grabbed their suitcases, eager for a tip, and trotted off with them in the direction of the station exit. Rats scuttled. Behind them, the latticed compartments of the huffing train rolled out of the station again.

"Poona, at the time, was very primitive," my mother told me.

They lived, at first, at the Poona Turf Club. It was a leftover from the 1920s, when horse races were popular among the British forces under the

Raj. By now, the billiards room, the card room and the ballroom had seen its wear, particularly after the monsoon season left mildew on drapes and cushions. The rooms, though sparse in number, were somewhat ventilated and in the evenings, there was the stir of a cooling breeze on the terrace.

"We lived there for a while," my mother recounted, "until we moved into a small, modest house surrounded by a dirt garden with young sapling trees that looked more like shrubs. It was not the beautiful bungalow I envisioned, but it served our needs."

It was leased to them by a doctor, furnished with black wicker furniture and slowly rotating fans on the ceiling. The house came with George, the cook, who had learned his culinary skills in a hotel in Bombay. George promptly fell in love with Thomas, the baby, whom he kept by his side at all times. When he pedaled to the market, Thomas came along, tucked into his bicycle basket. When George cooked in the kitchen, he placed Thomas on the tiled floor next to him and fed him dates and papayas.

"The heat was terrible," my mother remembered. "The baby's mattress was always damp with perspiration. In the evenings we moved him out onto the terrace where it was cooler and put chairs on either side of him so he wouldn't roll off the bed."

After nightfall, when my parents retired to bed, the night watchman, with skin so dark it offset his white turban and equally white single tooth, walked around the house at hourly intervals. He pounded on the surrounding shrubs and trees with a wooden pole in order to scare away snakes.

I listened, half in horror, half in awe.

"Your father started working at the Institute," my mother continued. "Every day seemed to present us with something new. It was all new and exciting to us."

She told me about peddlers from Kashmir who wandered house to house in the mornings to sell cloth and carpets from a huge trunk they carried with them. She described sticky Indian sweets, and the ducks that George kept in a baby pool in the garden, and the *ayah* who mopped the tiles meticulously but refused to clean toilets because that was work for "untouchables." At the peak of summer my parents fled to Mahableshwar, a hill station south of Poona, where the elevation provided cooler temperatures and strawberries grew in abundance. She described Diwali, a five-day festival of lights, when small clay lamps were filled with oil and kept illuminated during the night to proclaim the triumph of good over evil.

Her smile was soft as she reminisced.

"I think you were awfully brave," I told her after listening for a while. "To make yourself a home in a land where everything was foreign and unfamiliar and frightening, where you had to take such risks."

"But you did the same," she answered. "You went to Alaska, didn't you?"

I thought back on our decision to move north, to a place remote and disquieting and thrilling. We had plunged forward, kindled by the vigor of our youth and the draw of an exciting new place, just like my parents did when they went to India. It was an adventure we embarked upon eagerly, one we felt we could shape. We were undaunted. We trusted ourselves to chance.

How different it was with my transplant. It was a risk taken in tremor and fear, unrelenting and without choice. I had not felt courage. I did not try to be heroic. Life gave me no other option. Diminished, I clawed from one morning to the next, hour by hour, afraid to look far into the future. I tried not to think beyond the next day because the weight and uncertainty of the future could so easily crumble me. It was an effort at self-preservation, instinctual and necessary. Nothing more.

When I glanced back at my mother, I knew her thoughts had followed mine.

She looked at me for a long while before she said, "I was not nearly as brave as you."

CHAPTER 41

Letter from My Donor

The first letter arrived a month after my transplant. It was delivered to our mailbox in the lobby. I looked at the lettering and saw that it was from the donor center, forwarded to me by the Seattle Cancer Care Alliance's transplant search coordinator. A letter from my donor.

The envelope had travelled far. My donor held the same piece of paper in her hands, crisp between her fingers. It was carefully creased and folded. She had written the words within it. In that moment she was no longer an abstract entity to me but the very person that had sent my transplant in motion. She was the one behind my ability to take my next breath. With a trembling hand, I ripped open the envelope.

It was typed in German, needlessly translated for me into English, and consisted of a mere paragraph:

Dear Recipient,

    It is a matter of great concern for me to write this letter today. I hope you don't mind that I want to get in touch with you. It is not easy for me to put my thoughts into words. I want to wish you strength, courage and stamina in the coming weeks and months. I hope so much that you will be well again and win the battle against leukemia. I think of you every day and wish you all the best from the bottom of my heart. I do not know your present condition or state of mind. I am writing to wish you all the strength and stamina you need to conquer this disease. I hope that you are well enough to be able to read my letter.

                                              Many regards,
                                              Your donor.

I read the letter many times over. I wandered over to the window and read it again. I took it with me to my bedroom where I paced the floor before reading it a third time. Finally, I placed it on my bedside table next to a photograph of my family. The picture was taken on our last holiday on the island of Skopelos in Greece, the summer right before my diagnosis. I sat on the edge of my bed and stared at both the letter and the photograph. I was afraid to write back. I thought back on the summer when perhaps an "evil eye" had been cast upon me, as many Greeks believe when misfortune falls. I did not want my recuperation arrested by premature victory cries, as though writing to my donor with jubilant claims of success might bring the disease back into my life.

How delicate our situation was to that compared to other transplant patients and organ donors. In such situations, correspondence from a recipient would surely induce torment for the family of a deceased organ donor. One family waited and prayed for the member of another family to die. When word was given that an organ was available, it was only because a future was possible for another when someone else's life had failed. One life was renewed while the other was shadowed and lost. It was a time for both rejoicing and for despair. What rationale could be provided to justify the loss of a loved one for the continued life of a stranger?

My donor and I: we were different. We were both still alive. I owed this woman my life. I was able to think about her, to conjure thoughts about her decision and kindness, to wonder where she might live and prosper. What had prompted her to give me such a gift? Would I ever know?

I took the letter back to the living room and sat down with it at the wooden table. I reached for my notepad, twirling my pen, hesitant to lay its tip to paper. Would I ever gain back my confidence? Would there ever be a time when I would think that I was also still deserving of a long life ahead?

My mother came to stand beside me with a questioning look. "Will you write back?"

"I don't know if I can find the words to thank her," I told her.

Finally, I composed a letter:

Liebe Spenderin,

mit viel Freude habe ich deine Zeilen erhalten. Ich denke, ich darf dich jetzt du-zen, weil wir ja durch deine Stammzellen fast verwandt sind. Ich kann berichten, dass die Transplantation vor fünf Wochen sehr gut erfolgt ist. Meine neuen Zellen sind eifrig dabei, sich in ihrem neuen zu Hause zurechtzufinden. Bisher läuft alles bestens. Ich weiß nicht, wie ich mich bei dir für dein Geschenk bedanken soll.

I translated my thoughts onto paper:

Dear Donor,

With much joy I received your letter. I feel as though I am related to you through your stem cells; therefore, I wonder if I can address you informally as "du." I can gladly report to you that I am recuperating after the transplant five weeks ago. Your stem cells are working in my favor and are trying to establish themselves in their new home. I am progressing. I don't know how I can express the gratitude I feel in my heart for the gift you gave me.

I wanted to continue, to share with her the details of my life before leukemia, to tell her about my children and my husband and my home in Alaska. She needed to understand that her gift was not just one she made to me but to all of us. I had to write anonymously, as dictated by the donor bank etiquette. I understood the reason for this strictly imposed namelessness. My fragile condition could deteriorate at any moment. One year would have to pass before I would even be allowed to ask for her identity. Before then, the donor bank rationale went, I could too easily succumb to my own vulnerability.

One thing I knew about her, though, was that she was from Germany. I thought about the country I had left long ago. I had lived in America for so many years now that my homeland sometimes felt like an echo of another life. Over the course of the years, I had come to love the ease and amiability of the American people. Living in different cities and towns, in Ohio and Missouri and Alaska, I learned to cherish the differing landscapes they offered. Together with Nick, I embarked on the adventure life in America had in store for us. Our children were born here. We were home.

But I still felt bound to another world across the sea where my parents and brothers and sister found their calling. Sometimes I felt a pang of regret for having chosen to go to America in the first place, for falling in love with its fantastic, extravagant breadth and the man I would eventually marry. It was a decision made quickly, buzzing with thrill. A letter of application was mailed to Oberlin College. When a favorable response arrived from a college in a country where I had never set foot, I was on my way, tripping over myself in excitement, ready to start my life as a student. I never imagined that I would live for twenty-six years away from the home that built me and the people I came from.

Occasionally, I felt the unequivocal urge to return to Germany. I had never given up my German passport, as though its pages would forever bind me to the country I left so long ago. I made great efforts to teach my children my native language. Now and again, we journeyed back to Füssen in southern Bavaria. We spent summer days swimming in cold Alpine lakes and bicycled through scenery reminiscent of my children's fairy tale books. When it came time to return to America I did so with a favorable inclination but not without the sense that I was leaving a little part of me behind.

And now, through an unknown donor from Germany, my past beckoned and held out a hand to help me cross a crevasse. The trust in my heritage was cemented once more. I had never abandoned it, and it had never abandoned me.

CHAPTER 42
Seattle Sunshine

"Do you happen to have a dollar?" a homeless woman on Minor Avenue asked of a passerby.

My sister Andrea and I hung over the balcony railing, peering down. The bag lady wore thick woolen socks with sandals despite the warmth of the summer evening. Her skirt was grimy, her overcoat tattered at the elbows. Her darting eyes held the look of distraction. She was in a world of her own.

A man, smartly dressed, dug into his trouser pocket for change. Irritation creased his forehead as he dropped coins into her outstretched palm. He circled wide around her as he hurried on.

"Do you think she'll buy food with it?" I wondered out loud.

The woman sat down curbside, trailed her fingers into the gutter and found the end of a cigarette. She wedged the cigarette butt behind her ear. We watched her progress. On the corner of Minor and Republican she approached another couple, this time a man and woman with a child in a stroller.

"Do you happen to have a dollar?"

"She'll make a fortune at the rate she's going," Andrea commented. She turned to me. "I say we go to the barbeque at the SCCA House tonight."

We had seen the flyer posted in the elevator earlier that week. It was a barbeque organized by the American Cancer Society. Attendees could include anyone afflicted with cancer if they were well enough to attend, as well as their caregivers. A gathering in the sterilized dining hall, with hamburgers and potato salad and coleslaw, bound to go to waste because of underdeveloped appetites. Bald heads, fatigued eyes, the swapping of cancer stories. I was not holding my breath. Andrea, eager to fill the long days and evenings we were confined to the apartment with any diversion, prodded me to go.

"It'll be a nice walk for you," she encouraged. "Plus, I need to see hamburgers the size of Jupiter. That's what America is famous for."

I reluctantly agreed.

My sister had arrived from Germany two weeks before as my final caretaker. I measured time in terms of the succession of caretakers; first Nick, then my mother, finally my sister. After Andrea's tenure, still a tract of time seemingly endless to me, I would be allowed to return to Alaska. For one hundred days I was confined to a reachable radius from the hospital. It was a distance short enough for me to return to its care should my condition suddenly take a turn for the worse. From my perch on the couch, I had become progressively more irritable. I was tired—of my lethargy, of feeling drained and uneasy, of my own enfeeblement.

"By the time Andrea arrives," Nick told me before he left for Alaska, "you should be well enough to leave the apartment. For walks or whatever your energy level allows you. It would be good for you. But you need to be very careful still. Try to avoid crowded indoor spaces."

I scowled at him. I wanted my old life back. Even the book I had sifted through absentmindedly was propped spine up for days. My eyes were too tired to focus. My thoughts remained scattered. My enthusiasm wilted. Where was the woman from before, engaged in her studies, stimulated by college seminar discussions, tirelessly learning everything she possibly could? What had become of the person who studied well into the dark of night, immersed in research for her Ph.D.?

"Have you read Umberto Eco's semiotic theories of sign interpretation in linguistics?" I asked Nick at the dinner table. "I think it can be applied to art."

He sat, listening.

"They can be used to interpret art. The same concepts, the same language. Maybe I can construct a model for using them to understand works of art."

Nick smiled at my enthusiasm.

I didn't merely smile. I knew I could do it.

Nothing proved to be too difficult in those days: graduate seminars, commuting an hour to Columbus for work every day at the Wexner Center for the Arts, maintaining our first home together, finding time to cook dinner. Even after Yanni was born and I was endlessly walking up and down the length of the hallway, swaying him to sleep in my arms while slackened from lack of sleep myself, I simply told myself that I would have to finish my dissertation before he learned how to walk. That's all.

But now, I was deflated and spent. My time in Seattle was slowly drawing to a close. A beacon of light at the end of the long tunnel should have lifted me. Still, I felt reduced and brought down to my knees. Surviving the bone marrow transplant was the most difficult thing I had ever attempted to do. It was an ascent of Denali, the highest peak in North America, by the precarious West Buttress Route in the middle of an Alaskan winter. Every prior endeavor by comparison, however ambitious at the time, now seemed diminutive, secondary and insignificant.

I knew I needed to bolster my outlook, to reinforce my earlier fortitude and wring myself back to normal. But I was not sure how. It was when I found myself in such throes that Andrea arrived.

Grudgingly, I agreed to her suggestions and left the apartment for outings. A stroll took us to nearby Cascade Park. A walk down to the waterfront of Lake Union allowed us to sit on a bench overlooking the water. Her presence shifted my mood a little. She tried to distract me from my illness, filling the days around transfusion appointments and wellness checks and blood draws with these digressions.

She bantered about the doctors and the clinic, turning them into a joke, wanting to see me smile.

"Here's Dr. Ibrahim," Andrea announced, grinning in anticipation, as we sat in a transfusion cubicle in the clinic and waited for the doctor on call.

Dr. Ibrahim, a resident doctor on loan from Egypt, became the particular target of our chaffing. With his doleful expression, diffident stance and glasses that continuously slipped down his nose, it was easy to poke fun at him. He made it all too evident to us that he was still fresh out of residency, uncertain of my treatment plan and hesitant to make decisions. When Nick was still in Seattle over the weekend, he stood with the nurse at the computer in my transfusion room, consulting with her rather than Dr. Ibrahim.

"*Schliesst ihn doch ein,*" Andrea grinned, muttering to me in German. *Come on, include him,* in the manner of an anxious mother on the playground wanting a group of children to include her awkward child in their games.

We smiled as we watched Dr. Ibrahim stand on tiptoe to peer over Nick's shoulder, desperate to see the computer screen as well.

"We lived in Egypt," Andrea began conversationally when Dr. Ibrahim came in. We had just learned of the doctor's homeland moments before. He shuffled distractedly through my chart, then blinked in disbelief.

"Really?" he asked, pushing his glasses up onto his nose. My chart was momentarily forgotten.

We had visited all the sites, we told him. We saw the pyramids on the Giza plateau, splendored against the desert horizon. We wandered through the Khan-el-Khalili bazaar, fragrant with spices and shisha pipes, vibrant with hanging carpets and tapestries. We rode on horseback through the sand dunes to the Saqqara Pyramid. We marveled at the Valley of the Kings and Queens in Thebes, where we walked through temples and tombs. The evening sun glowed amber above the desert. The presence of antiquity hung thick.

A nostalgic expression crossed Dr. Ibrahim's face. "You've really been there?" he asked us. He raised an eyebrow, not sure whether we were ridiculing him.

We both nodded, our expressions deliberately neutral. Dr. Ibrahim's glance darted between us, as though he was not sure what to make of us. Remembering the purpose of his visit, he busied himself with my chart. He removed some pages which he needed to "edit" and left the room.

Andrea and I looked at each other, giggling.

"Do you think he'll remember to return the pages to your chart?" Andrea asked me.

We both cackled, feeling just a little guilty about teasing poor Dr. Ibrahim. We were not concerned at all about my potentially incomplete chart.

On another occasion Andrea and I strolled across the campus of the

University of Washington. We kept to outdoor spaces, separating ourselves from hordes of students with backpacks. Near the center of campus, we came across a straggly tree which was conspicuously surrounded by a black iron fence and embellished with a plaque. The grafted cutting was a descendant of Newton's apple tree in England. Newton had supposedly sat beneath the original tree when hit simultaneously on the head by the apple and had his stroke of brilliant insight regarding the Earth's gravitational pull.

Andrea and I stood looking at it skeptically.

"Must be a true descendant," Andrea said, "for it to be located in such a great place of learning and wisdom."

Just a few steps farther down the university path, we came across a building named "Bloedel House." This sent us into fits of laughter again when we understood the irony of its presence among the formidable, red-brick university halls, particularly after just seeing Newton's tree of wisdom. Translated into German, the name implied a fool, an idiot, a silly bloke.

We reverted back to a time left behind, to juvenile banalities and joking, an easier life. Even serious matters, such as the need to nourish my seriously underweight body, were addressed lightheartedly. Before Nick left, he prodded me to eat constantly — blueberries or avocados or milkshakes. He lined up rows of healthy, whole grain cereals on the refrigerator, but the only cereal brand I had a taste for was Lucky Charms. Andrea immediately walked seven blocks to Whole Foods, searching its shelves in vain for the sugary cereal I craved. Disappointed, she returned. Then she met Phil, the shuttle bus driver, who pulled up in front of the Pete Gross House twice a day to pick up any resident wanting to go to Safeway for groceries. At Safeway she might be more successful, Phil reassured her. Andrea eagerly clambered onto the bus, returning with paper bags full of groceries. That evening we had a feast: asparagus risotto, bagels and lox, German pickles and Lucky Charms. Even though they were all thrown together haphazardly, I was able to stomach everything.

When we proudly told my nutritionist counselor about our culinary soiree the next day, she sourly reprimanded us for having consumed the lox. It was smoked, therefore undercooked, and still on my forbidden list. Crestfallen, we left.

When we got beyond earshot, I turned to Andrea and grinned. "Let's celebrate my last infusion on Day 96 at McDonald's!"

Andrea agreed at once.

Even if she could not make everything alright, Andrea unburdened the days that passed. She was still my fashion consultant, not so much in the manner of our childhood days, when we found our mother's shoes and skirts to dress up in. More subdued, she carefully tied my bandana to cover my bald head and straightened my blouse to cover the Hickman port line in my chest. She was still able to read my mind. When my thoughts drifted into dark places, she steered the conversation to neutral ground or pulled out her Kindle to read aloud to me. I noticed that since her arrival in Seattle three weeks ago, it had not rained even a single day.

With food on our minds again, quibbling as usual, we walked that evening to the barbeque at the SCCA House. Pigeons fluttered down from rooftops and settled on the sidewalk next to us.

"Don't breathe!" Andrea instructed sternly, as she had heard Nick tell me before. Pigeons carried diseases and harbored filth. "Don't breathe!"

I laughed. After all that I had come though, it seemed the antithesis of what I needed to do. Andrea, seeing my point, started laughing as well. The evening was balmy and calm. The walk down Minor Avenue was manageable. At Cascade Park, two men lazily threw a Frisbee between them in the waning light. Dahlias gently nodded their heads at us in the adjacent community garden.

While we waited for the elevator to take us to the second-floor kitchen and dining room of the SCCA House, the venue of tonight's barbeque, we noticed an announcement affixed to the wall between elevator doors.

Wedding Bells at the SCCA House.

A photograph showed the couple. White gown, tuxedo, a cascade of freesias in her hand. Their smiles were not completely unburdened. Bald heads, alabaster skin, lymphoma, esophageal cancer. They were making their time together count. I swallowed and pretended not to notice how Andrea quickly pressed the elevator button again.

The gathering in the dining room was subdued. Caregivers with exaggerated smiles kept up conversations with other caregivers equally desperate to be part of normal life again while patients silently pushed food around on their plates. I finished half a hot dog before my stomach revolted. Perhaps I should have stuck to the Ensure drinks and Gatorade that Nick had stockpiled into the kitchen cabinet at the apartment. I was glad for an excuse to escape.

On the rooftop garden back at the house, the evening had transitioned into shadows. Beyond the low wall of the rooftop patio, Seattle's cityscape glittered. The contours of buildings were etched sharply into the violet sky. In the opposite direction, Lake Union shimmered silver and tranquil. Andrea and I leaned back on wooden Adirondack chairs, ran our fingers through planters of brome hay and breathed in the night air. High above, an airliner followed its course through the night sky, leaving SeaTac airport for some distant destination. We watched it pass over us.

"I want to go home," Andrea and I said at the same time.

Unlike countless times in the past, when we were children and our minds found the same instant to cross paths, and we punched each other in the upper arm, yelling "Jinks!" this time we both fell silent. Any amount of bantering was not going to change the outcome of my ordeal. We could joke and laugh in the manner of our childhood days, but I would never have my old life again. It would never be as it was before. The burden of illness and uncertainty loomed beyond my stay in Seattle.

What did life have in store for the bag lady on the street, asking for quarters, near the "Home Deli" that catered to cancer patients and the homeless? Would she still be approaching strangers in years to come, long after I had returned home? And what would become of the couple that had wed in the SCCA House, brave enough to arrest time in order to cherish each other for the remainder of their days together? And of me, too afraid to leave Seattle and its prescribed circumference, the proximity of doctors and medications and help, as my time was slowly concluding?

CHAPTER 43
Chimera

Dear Donor,

    I will be returning to my life at home soon. It is difficult to believe that the long, hard time here is over and I will be at home again. I look forward to being reunited with my children. I am, however, filled with anxiety. While I must believe that your cells will allow me a normal life again, I think about the fragility of the future. Will time build my confidence again?

In dawn's transition to fuller day, the outlines of the apartment building across the street, sheathed in glass and clean lines, became lavender. I sat at the wooden kitchen table for hours, waiting. My packed suitcases stood by the front door. I was ready to return to Alaska on an afternoon flight.

    At my final clinic appointment, I had been given lengthy instructions for my follow-up care. I was to have weekly blood draws and bi-weekly appointments with my oncologist in Fairbanks. I needed to be watchful for signs of chronic graft-versus-host disease. I had to worry about my delicate skin, my receding gums, and respiratory infections. Sun exposure was dangerous. Secondary cancers would always be a concern. Guardedly, they told me I could return home.

    I stared at the words I had written. My donor was unknown to me. At the same time, she was connected to me in the most fundamental manner. She mattered to me on a cellular level.

    After my bone marrow transplant, Nick joked on the phone with his friends that I was twenty-one again, my donor's age. Particularly his male friends guffawed at the idea that now he would have to work hard at keeping up with my younger pace. Naturally, their jokes were directed at our amorous intimacy and centered on the fact that he was, now, more than twice my age. Sometime later, more seriously, I thought about their comments and of the donor whose much younger stem cells now caroused through my bone marrow and veins. Perhaps my connection to this unknown person was more than arbitrary.

It could so easily have failed. Obstacles beyond our control could have impeded our encounter. Biologically, the donor bank might never have found the matching of our cell types. Chronologically, she could have lived a generation earlier or later, never destined to meet up with me in our narrow window of opportunity. Historically, the Berlin Wall might have never fallen, and the reunification of Germany never occurred, thus keeping her, as I later learned of her origins in the former East Germany, at a distance from me.

But it did happen.

She was my genetic twin. Through my transplant, I had become her blood chimera. Like the fire-breathing creature in Greek mythology that had the physical traits of a lion and a goat, I was now an individual made up of different genetic constitutions. Two different sets of DNA housed within me. After my own diseased bone marrow had been destroyed by chemotherapy, my donor's healthy marrow was put in its place. Her marrow, encrypted with her DNA, continued to make red blood cells. For the rest of my life, I would have blood cells that are genetically identical to that of my donor, but different from the rest of the cells in my body.

I was, truly, an individual made up of two halves. A before. And an after. Like the chimera of our blood, I was comprised of two persons: my former self before cancer and the being I had become after my ordeal. I was a changed person, at once craving the life I had led before my illness yet sensing deep inside that I would never be that person again.

One day, I would travel to Germany with the identity of my donor in hand. I would stand before her, together with Nick and Yanni and Helen, and present her with a bouquet of flowers even if it was a poor equivalent for her efforts. My embrace willed her to know that her magnanimity had turned all of our lives around. Our worlds had collided, unknowingly, unplanned for, extraordinarily.

I knew that even if this never happened, even if our letters faltered over time, the twisting of our fates was forever changed. My connection to her was solid. As destined as my blood type was to change from my own 0+ to her B+, so too was my firm belief that our consanguinity was inevitable.

One day I would thank those who had known me in my previous life. They regarded me differently even though they treated me as they did before. Some asked after my wellbeing, hesitantly inquiring about my chances of success. Others averted their eyes uncomfortably, skirting my illness, unsure of how to approach me again.

I would forgive those who did not come to be at my side, whether by choice or circumstance. It was not their fault. Slowly and over time, I embraced them again. I could recall the years we had already lived through, much longer than the time when I was afflicted with cancer. I relished the days we spent together when my illness had not defined me.

For the friends who supported me during my difficult time, I found no utterance to describe the indebtedness of my heart. I trusted that they understood me even with words left unsaid. I learned to heed small moments, inconspicuous events, subtle emotions. Matters that seemed important in my former life sifted away, tugged into the past. Of the two entities residing in my body, the one that lived before leukemia faded slowly into a background motif, a mosaic of beautiful colors. She lived another life, one I could not return to, but would be etched into me forever.

The other me soldiered on. Branded as I was by my illness, I found my refuge, humbled by gratitude, finally understanding the saying that it is not what life deals you that matters but the grace with which you accommodate it that is important.

I returned to my home, lifted by my children's tight embrace and by the look in my husband's eyes when I met his gaze over their heads.

And we shed sacred tears together.

EPILOGUE
Beyond Boreas

In the boreal forest that surrounds our home in Alaska, Nick and I walk with the dog on a softened, pine-needle strewn trail. The air is crisp, invigorating, our breaths drawn deep and cold. The coniferous forest, thick with birches and spruces and larches, has turned auburn and yellow. It surrounds us in dappled, striated light falling through the remaining leaves.

We walk in silence with the sound of the wind in our ears, a long, drawn-out rushing sound when it gets caught in the spread of the spruces. The dog bounds ahead, sniffing, straying from the trail. Contrary to our typical route, the landscape presents itself to us from a different angle today. The trail ahead of us twists, the birches unfamiliar, the carpet of white dwarf dogwoods on the forest floor spread in an altered manner. The dog, hesitant in his usual instinct to take the left fork, looks back at us. He whines at the uncertain path.

I, too, was veered off course. I was forced onto a detour where everything looked precarious and frightening. Ironically, cancer shaped my path and steered me to a place familiar and safe again. I am part of this northern landscape. I found within it purpose and comfort when I lost my sense of direction. It uprooted me. Then it balanced me again.

I smile at the dog and motion him forward. There is nothing to worry about. The boreal forest lies in front of us. In the Greek myth, the tale of Boreas unfolds. The North Wind hurls his fierce, icy winds from the northern mountains of Thrace. He sends discomfort and hardship to the people living below. Beyond Boreas, however, lies another land, named Hyperborea. It is a beautiful and temperate land where old age is unknown. Its people are blessed with longevity and happiness.

I look around me at the bright yellow leaves of the birches sifting gently to the forest floor, at the evergreens standing tall, at the glittering light as it falls through the forest.

I am, quite possibly, already there.

ACKNOWLEDGMENTS

I wrote *Transplanted* several years after I underwent my bone marrow transplant. Before then, the content was too raw to process into a manuscript. Putting my experience into words was an unimaginably therapeutic process. I'm grateful to so many for helping me write this story.

To early draft readers –Gloria Kempton, Michael Lennertz, Tara Bellion, Rebecca Henderson, Joan Braddock -- thank you for your careful reading and your constant encouragement.

To fellow writers and writing group critique partners -- Lyssa Reese, Anne Winchell and Crystal Taggart -- for kindling ideas, suggesting alternatives and for many inspiring discussions.

I want to thank my editor, Michael Burwell, and my publisher, Sandra Kleven at Cirque Press for wanting my story, for thoughtful editing and for making my book a reality.

I am indebted to the doctors and nurses at the University of Washington Medical Center, the Seattle Cancer Care Alliance and the Fairbanks Cancer Care Physicians. Without them I would, quite literally, never have written this book.

I relied on and researched valuable sources that informed the book. Whether in the form of medical terminology, the natural phenomena of the northern landscape or the history of Interior Alaska, I looked to many sources for guidance and consulted them in telling the story. I have cited them in a bibliography at the end of the book.

To my heroic friends Tara and Rebecca, for being so solidly there.

To my husband Nick, for gently prodded me to write the story, knowing me so well that he understood my need to shout out the story at a time when I could barely whisper. For his support and love I am forever grateful. Thank you for being in my life.

Most of all to my children, Yanni and Helen, who gave me a reason to keep going at a time when the world stopped turning.

BIBLIOGRAPHY

"Alaska." *Online Etymology Dictionary: Origin, history and meaning of English words.* https://www.etymology.com/word/alaska (accessed September 20, 2017).

"Acute Myeloid Leukemia (AML): Your Chances for Recovery (Prognosis)." University of Rochester Health Encyclopedia. https://www.urmc.rochester.edu/healthencyclopedia (accessed October 24, 2018).

Beelsebub and L. Atwood. "The Spiritual Meaning of the Autumn Equinox." *The Path of the Spiritual Sun: Celebrating the solstices and equinoxes.* Mystical Life Publications Ltd, 2011.

Bonnell, R. "The Tanana River's historic role as a transportation route." *Fairbanks Daily News Miner.* https://www.newsminer.com, April 8, 2017 (accessed November 4, 2018).

"Boreas: Horses, Hyperborea and the North Wind." https://earthandstarryheaven.com, November 2, 2016 (accessed September 20, 2018).

Buxton, M. "Koyukuk man recalls early mushing life." *Fairbanks Daily News Miner,* March 13, 2017.

Cole, D. *Historic Fairbanks: An Illustrated History.* San Antonio, TX: Historical Publishing Network, 2002, pp. 5-6.

Damaschke, S. "Dismantling the myth of the 'Trümmerfrauen'" https://www.dw.com. Deutsche Welle /Germany/DW/24.11/2014 (accessed January 14, 2018).

Davis. N. *The Aurora Watcher's Handbook.* Fairbanks, AK: University of Alaska Press, 1992, pp. 4-7.

Engel, M. "The successes kept you going." *Hutch Magazine*, Vol. 38, No. 3, 2015, p. 5.

"Granulocyte colony stimulating factor (G-CSF), https://www.cancerresearchuk.org, August 4, 2014 (accessed February 16, 2017).

Jokinen, A. "Aurora Borealis, The Northern Lights in Mythology and Folklore." Luminarium. www.luminarium.org/mythology/revontulet.htm (accessed August 22, 2017).

Helfferich, C. "Aurora Season." Alaska Science Forum, Article 1046, Alaska Science Forum, Geophysical Institute, University of Alaska Fairbanks. https://www.gi.alaska.edu/science forum, September 4, 1991 (accessed March 18, 2017).

Hesse, H. *Bäume: Betrachtungen und Gedichte*. Frankfurt am Main: Insel Verlag, 1984.

Khan, F., Agarwal, A. & Agrawal, S. "Significance of chimerism in hematopoietic stem cell transplantation: new variations on an old theme." *Bone Marrow Transplantation*. 34, (2004), pp. 1-14.

Kher, A. "Atmospheric phenomena: Halos, sundogs and light pillars." https://www.timeanddate.com/astronomy/optical-phenomenon.html. Time and Date AS 1995- 2016 (accessed November 23, 2016).

Klastersky, J., J. de Naurois, K. Rolston, B. Rapoport, G. Maschmeyer, M. Aapro, & J. Herrstedt. "Management of Febrile Neutropenia: ESMO Clinical Practice Guidelines." *Annals of Oncology*, Vol. 27, Issue 5, 2016.

"Leukemia: Cancer Institute Overview. Cleveland Clinic. https://myclevelandclinic.org/health/articles/leukemia-cancer-overview (accessed January 25, 2017).

Lilly. "Omens and Prophecies: Rainbow halo around the sun" Nature Blessings. https://Psychicsspiritinyou.com/omens-and-prophesies-rainbowhalo-around the sun, 28 February 2014 (accessed November 23, 2016).

Mayo, W. "Introduction." *Alaska native ways: What the elders have taught us.* Portland, OR: Graphic Arts Center Publishing, 2002, p. 14.

"Mushers' Guide to the Yukon Quest trail." www.yukonquest.com/race-central/yukon-quest -trail/yukon-quest-trail-map (accessed November 22, 2017).

"Myths of the Aurora." *Fairbanks Daily News Miner.* H-13. December 9, 2001.

Praderlo, C. "It's possible for one person to have two different sets of DNA- here's how it happens." https://www.thisisinsider.com/what-is-a-human-chimera-and-how-does-it-happen-, Nov. 6, 2017 (accessed September 3, 2018).

Rettner, R. "3 Human Chimeras that already exist." https://www.livescience.com, August 5, 2016 (accessed September 3, 2018).

Rozell, N. "Ice dies, fire survives in Interior Alaska." Article 1749. Alaska Science Forum, Geophysical Institute, University of Alaska Fairbanks. https://www.gi.alaska.science, May 5, 2005 (accessed December 8, 2016).

Rozell. N. "Diamond dust dazzles on dog days.'" Alaska Science Forum, Geophysical Institute, University of Alaska, Fairbanks. https://www.gi.alaska.edu/science forum, April 7, 2019 (accessed September 5, 2020).

"Rupture in South-Central Alaska – The Denali Fault Earthquake of 2002." USGS Fact Sheet 014-03. Compiled by G S. Fuis and L. A. Wald. Edited by J. W. Hendley II and P. H. Stauffer. https://pubs.usgs.gov, Feb 5, 2003 (accessed May 15, 2017).

Sekeres, M.A. and M. King. "Acute Myeloid Leukemia." Cleveland Clinic Center for Continuing Education. https://clevelandclinicmeded.com, April 2014.

Tobia, M. "Sun dogs light up the sky." Times News Online. www.tnonline.com/2014/aug/09/sun-dogs-light-sky (accessed April 23, 2016).

Waller, D. *RavenTales: Stories of the Raven based on the folklore of the Tlingit, Haida, Tsimshian, Inuit and Athapascan of Alaska*, 2014.

Wallis, V. *Two Old Women*. Seattle, WA: Epicenter Press, 1993.

Webster, D.H and W. Zibell. *Inupiat-Eskimo dictionary*. Fairbanks, AK: Summer Institute of Linguistics, 1970. https://library.alaska.gov/hist (accessed January 20, 2019).

Williams, B. *Ethics and the Limits of Philosophy*. Cambridge, MA: Harvard University Press, 1985, pp. 69-70.

ABOUT THE AUTHOR

Birgit Lennertz Sarrimanolis holds a BA in art history and German studies, an MA in art history, and a PhD in art education. Her work has appeared in *Cirque Journal, Five on the Fifth, 49 Writers, Shark Reef,* and *Medicine and Meaning.* Her story "April Supermoon" aired on Juneau KTOO's Community Connections series. She was a finalist in the 2020 Pacific Northwest Writers Association literary contest and won second place in the 2021 Annual Writer's Digest Writing Competition. She regularly attends writing conferences, including the Pacific Northwest Writers Conference, the Seattle Writing Workshop, and the Kachemak Bay Writers Conference. She has lived in Indonesia, India, Chile, Argentina, Egypt, Germany, and Greece, but now calls Alaska home, where she writes overlooking the Tanana Valley. More information and her Alaskan blog can be found at her website: www.birgitsarrimanolis.com

ABOUT CIRQUE PRESS

Cirque Press grew out of *Cirque*, a literary journal that publishes the works of writers and artists from the North Pacific Rim, a region that reaches north from Oregon to the Yukon Territory, south through Alaska to Hawaii, and west to the Russian Far East.

Cirque Press is a partnership of Sandra Kleven, publisher, and Michael Burwell, editor. Ten years ago, we recognized that works of talented writers in the region were going unpublished, and the Press was launched to bring those works to fruition. We publish fiction, nonfiction, and poetry, and we seek to produce art that provides a deeper understanding about the region and its cultures. The writing of our authors is significant, personal, and strong.

Sandra Kleven – Michael Burwell, publishers and editors
www.cirquejournal.com

BOOKS FROM CIRQUE PRESS

Apportioning the Light by Karen Tschannen (2018)

The Lure of Impermanence by Carey Taylor (2018)

Echolocation by Kristin Berger (2018)

Like Painted Kites & Collected Works by Clifton Bates (2019)

Athabaskan Fractal: Poems of the Far North by Karla Linn Merrifield (2019)

Holy Ghost Town by Tim Sherry (2019)

Drunk on Love: Twelve Stories to Savor Responsibly by Kerry Dean Feldman (2019)

Wide Open Eyes: Surfacing from Vietnam by Paul Kirk Haeder (2020)

Silty Water People by Vivian Faith Prescott (2020)

Life Revised by Leah Stenson (2020)

Oasis Earth: Planet in Peril by Rick Steiner (2020)

The Way to Gaamaak Cove by Doug Pope (2020)

Loggers Don't Make Love by Dave Rowan (2020)

The Dream That Is Childhood by Sandra Wassilie (2020)

Seward Soundboard by Sean Ulman (2020)

The Fox Boy by Gretchen Brinck (2021)

Lily Is Leaving: Poems by Leslie Ann Fried (2021)

One Headlight by Matt Caprioli (2021)

November Reconsidered by Marc Janssen (2021)

Callie Comes of Age by Dale Champlin (2021)

Someday I'll Miss This Place Too by Dan Branch (2021)

Out There In The Out There by Jerry McDonnell (2021)

Fish the Dead Water Hard by Eric Heyne (2021)

Salt & Roses by Buffy McKay (2022)

Growing Older In This Place: A Life in Alaska's Rainforest by Margo Wasserman Waring (2022)

Kettle Dance: A Big Sky Murder by Kerry Dean Feldman (2022)

Nothing Got Broke by Larry F. Slonaker (2022)

On the Beach: Poems 2016-2021 by Alan Weltzien (2022)

Sky Changes on the Kuskokwim by Clifton Bates (2022)

Transplanted by Birgit Lennertz Sarrimanolis (2022)

Yosemite Dawning by Shauna Potocky (2022)

Between Promise and Sadness by Joanne Townsend (2022)

Infinite Meditations: For Inspiration and Daily Practice by Scott Hanson (2022)

CIRCLES
Illustrated books from Cirque Press

Baby Abe: A Lullaby for Lincoln by Ann Chandonnet (2021)

Miss Tami, Is Today Tomorrow? by Tami Phelps (2021)

Miss Bebe Goes to America by Lynda Humphrey (2022)

More Praise for *Transplanted*

In *Transplanted*, Birgit Lennertz Sarrimanolis presents her definitive, vivid journey through the darkest moments of a near-death diagnosis, set against the beauty of Alaska. Once you begin, there is no other choice but to follow this writer on her path. It seems so every day—that one backache could catapult you into life-and-death chaos. And yet, even with the grave danger of her illness, Sarrimanolis tempers her narrative with the glittering panorama of her home state and what led up to her being airlifted to Seattle for emergency treatment...With her lustrous descriptions of her family, sparkling snows, sunsets, and joyful romps across rugged terrain, it's clear that the magic of community, land, and sky plays a dominant role in her story. In every word of her frank, gorgeous prose, readers will discover what it means to heal and truly thrive, no matter what life throws at you.

– Patience Bloom, author of *Romance is My Day Job*

A memoir of a transplant's life in Alaska, including a fight against leukemia...This book presents two parallel yet intersecting stories of living in the frozen North and facing down the possibility of death...She speaks of the hardships of an Alaskan winter but also its joys...Her clear appreciation of Alaska's natural wonders makes her accounts of the necessary isolation during treatment all the more poignant...In addition to the physical trials, Sarrimanolis ably recounts her emotional trials, including those relating to her relationships with family and friends. Throughout much of the book, the author recounts a grim story, with descriptions of treatments that make the upbeat ending seem almost jarring...a gripping narrative...A harrowing but uplifting story of cancer survival.

– Kirkus Reviews

www.ingramcontent.com/pod-product-compliance
Lightning Source LLC
LaVergne TN
LVHW061610070526
838199LV00078B/7230